Volcanic Momentum

GET THINGS DONE BY SETTING DESTINY GOALS, MASTERING THE ENERGY CODE, AND NEVER LOSING STEAM

JORDAN RING

Publishing services provided by  **Archangel Ink**

ISBN-13: 978-1-942761-91-4

DEDICATION

This book is dedicated to the standup team at Archangel Ink. Without Rob and Kristie I never would have gotten this far with my writing, book marketing, and all my book-related items. I thank you both for your candid feedback during the titling process, your help with the formatting and cover design for this book, and for the countless life conversations that have served to bolster my real-world confidence.

The pleasure is mine when it comes to growing this company into the number-one publishing service for self-published authors everywhere.

Thank you for your friendship. Thank you for your time. Thank you for the chance to be a part of such an amazing team.

—Jordan

FOREWORD

It's common knowledge that nothing gives you more credibility as a writer than having your wife write your foreword.

Alright, it's not common knowledge at all, but Jordan's not common and that's what makes this book exceptional.

Let's flash back to 2015 for a moment, the year of the *The Force Awakens*, pizza rat, and Hotline Bling. In that year Jordan discovers a tribe of people leaving conventional employment to make money online. He realizes this is what he wants to do and pitches me his idea. I (being the supportive wife that I am) say, "Sure honey, go play on your computer."

Little did I know how serious he was about this goal or how far it would take us. Flash forward to 2018, the year of the royal wedding and *Rewrite the Stars*. Jordan has five self-published books, three online courses, four blogs, and assists other self-publishing authors to get their books out there.

As neither a writer nor a scholar (and as an obviously biased source), I have a very small platform of credibility on which to stand. Where my credibility lies is in the honor and pleasure of witnessing first hand Jordan's transformation into a man of action, goal setting, and legacy building.

I have had the distinct privilege of listening to Jordan's words for the past eight years and this has indubitably made me a better person. Jordan is a dreamer. Like bed bugs, dreams are contagious. I went from thinking "What's a goal?" and "I'm only passionate about naps and chocolate," to actively pursuing an entrepreneurial lifestyle and multiple goals simultaneously.

But this book isn't about Jordan or me. It's about you. You have goals to accomplish and things to get done. You have distractions and time-sucks. You're looking for info to propel you towards your dreams. You picked up this book in the hopes that it would equip you for the real world.

Self-improvement books typically fall into two traps. Number one is the overdependence on big-picture clichés such as "Change the world," "Get up and make a difference," and "Carpe diem." These phrases, while inspiring, lack an actionable response for the reader. Sure, I'd love to change the world today, but my couch is cozy and I haven't rewatched *The Office* in a couple of months.

The second danger is a book overflowing with hyper-specific habits, tiny details like "clip your nails on Thursdays," and unhelpful suggestions to set an alarm on your phone to go to bed. These life changes are great but without a larger vision for what you're trying to accomplish these changes come and go like the fashionability of mom jeans.

Jordan's skill lies in espousing fundamental big-picture truths with clear, concise direction. Focusing on the main motivations and short-comings of humanity is essential, and so is applying steps that can be taken immediately. Without Destiny Goals, our positive action steps lead us nowhere. Without taking steps, our goals lay dormant, unfulfilled, and visible on the horizon but never quite within reach.

Jordan knows how to nudge the lazy, encourage the weary, and awaken the passive.

But don't take my word for it. Read this book and watch how it changes your life.

Too many people in today's society are listlessly meandering through life without purpose and direction. Don't sell yourself short in life. Dream bigger dreams. Aim higher than you ever thought possible! Utilize the tools in this book to achieve those dreams and build (are you ready for it?)...Volcanic Momentum!

—Miranda

CONTENTS

Introduction:
THE POWER OF CHANGE

In the spring of 2015 my wife and I took a giant leap forward. We committed to moving "down south."

We had never before talked about moving anywhere other than within Pennsylvania. It just wasn't something we'd discussed. The thought was so vague and foreign we had no idea what it truly meant to us at the time.

But you know what? We went. We took a risk and dove right in. It meant going wherever the wind took us, hoping and trusting we would make it through. It meant believing that everything would work out despite some major trepidations to the contrary.

The big move started with a normal walk through our lovely town of Mechanicsburg, Pennsylvania. We had taken hundreds of similar walks in our four years of living there after graduating from college. This walk didn't seem like much of a change from the norm, but it ended up changing our lives.

During our regular five-mile loop we were suddenly struck with a desire to move away and start fresh. It hit both of us at the same time and we couldn't help but feel elated and expectant towards our future.

We came back from the walk, frightened yet exhilarated at the thought of starting over in a new place. It felt monumental and a little bit more than coincidence that we were both thinking the same thing.

Six months later, we were driving down to Atlanta, Georgia with a carload of stuff, embarking on a new adventure. We both became assistant managers in a retirement community and had to scramble to keep up with the fast-paced and ever-changing environment we found ourselves in.

We had each other, and that was it. Just Jordan and Miranda.

At the job we were on call four nights a week, served meals to residents in the dining room when staff didn't show up, and worked extremely late nights. This instilled a deep sense of hard work, and also a "what the heck were we thinking?!" type of mindset.

It was grueling work and we wanted to quit several times. Looking back, I'm not sure how (or why) we decided to keep going. But we did, and it ended up being one of the most rewarding decisions of our lives. This was our first step in moving towards volcanic momentum.

We were working towards our vision, even though that vision had not yet been made clear to us.

It's funny what you remember looking back. When I picture myself vacuuming the huge dining room at the retirement community, I now get a sense of nostalgia. There's nothing like that feeling: when you look back at a memory and instill it with positive feelings, even if, at the time, you'd wanted to be anywhere else.

How often is that the case? How often do we want to be somewhere else, when we really need to appreciate the here-and-now and learn to be present?

It's in this presence of mind that we can fight our way towards our goals. When we find ourselves vacuuming the same floor over and over again, while all we really want to do is work towards a big goal, we need to realize that the work we are doing now is preparing the way for us, no matter what that work is. Of course, we don't need to do the same work forever. But it's critical to become mindful of how your current situation is stimulating positive growth.

What I've realized is that the key to finding success is enjoying the moments along the way. Grasping long-term momentum is often about acceptance of menial tasks and an enduring commitment to seeing your dreams through to the end. Sustained and lasting momentum is found by maximizing the everyday moments and capitalizing on the time you do have.

You wouldn't think for a second that my goal of being a full-time writer was moving forward while I was vacuuming up the same mess at Table 3 over and over again. I sure didn't think so! But so it was.

I was learning to appreciate that getting to the end and completing a goal involves much more than I ever expected. It involves having an unparalleled commitment to see it through to the end.

This book is about keeping your head above water when the goal appears to be within reach, but still remains so far away. It's for those that are vacuuming, bussing tables, or working three jobs, and feel like you are just wasting time.

You aren't!

Reaching the right goal is worth the hard work, and I know you can do it! My hope is that the tips, tactics, and strategies in this book will propel you forward and allow you to bust through to your goal and go beyond.

But my heart is to encourage and uplift you if you're spending most of your time not seemingly working towards a goal. Everyone's busy and has a lot going on in their lives.

This book is meant to be in your hands if:

- You are ten pounds away from your ideal weight (I won't share dieting tips in this book, but the material is still highly relevant).

- You just made a major life change and you're freaking out, wondering if you made the right decision.

- You love what you do, but you're starting to feel empty at work, and are filled with a desire to dedicate more time to a side hustle or hobby.

- You know exactly what your goals are but find it hard to finish out goals to completion.

- You desire the better and more fulfilled life that comes when you start to crush all the goals before you.

- If you are way ahead of most of us and have a solid array of accomplishments behind you, congrats. I dare say you might still learn something here in terms of tactics related to continuing to work towards goals through difficult times. Or;

- You don't even know what you're working towards.

If any of the above is true for you, welcome to Volcanic Momentum! We are going to cover goal setting (specifically in terms of setting Destiny Goals), master the nine strategies to sustained momentum (including how to manage our time), and learn how we can keep on rolling and never lose steam.

The exercises in this book will clarify your goals and open up doors to possibilities you never imagined. It will show you that you have the power to change your life nestled deep within. With the tools of

Volcanic Momentum you will be able to break free and make a major impact in the lives of others.

This book is split into three actionable sections:

1) The first section is all about setting a firm foundation for explosive growth. Together we will bust the neutral myth and discover how easy it can be to set individualized, life-changing goals.

2) Section two dives into the meat of the book, with advice on how to keep up momentum towards your goals. We will learn to master the energy code, create time through priority management, how to invite serendipity, and much more. This part of the book will no doubt beef up your skills in finishing out any goal as quickly and efficiently as possible.

3) In section three I will share encouragement and guide you in how to never again lose steam. The main concept of my approach is to learn to always ask the important questions of yourself and others in order to keep heading in the right direction. Together we will learn how to find our purpose in this one life.

The road will be bumpy, the challenges trying, and the vacuuming seemingly endless, but together we will make it to the end.

Let's get started.

—Jordan

Section One:
A FIRM FOUNDATION FOR EXPLOSIVE GROWTH

A Quick Win:
A LASER FOCUS

"You don't have to see the whole staircase,
just take the first step."

—Martin Luther King Jr.

I am sure you have heard the saying "less is more," but what does it actually mean? It turns out having less (less clutter, less distractions, even less goals) can make all the difference in your journey to goal completion.

If we learn to work less and instead focus on the most important activities, we can get more done by doing the right things. We need to say goodbye to sixty-hour workweeks (which studies show[1] don't increase productivity anyway) and learn to work smarter.

Working less generally provides a greater level of results by increasing our focus and our ability to do the task at hand.

The same need for less work goes for New Year's resolutions and goal setting in general. If we want to accomplish A, B, C, and D in a year, we will never get all of it done.

---

1 "Calculating Loss of Productivity Due to OT
Using Charts - Nov 2001 | Overtime | Workweek And
Weekend." https://www.scribd.com/document/75599238/
Calculating-Loss-of-Productivity-Due-to-OT-Using-Charts-Nov-2001.

What we need is a focus, a point of origin for all of our thoughts for the upcoming year. Whether it's the beginning of the year or the middle of summer when you are reading this book, you must pick a singular focus for growth to occur. Even the middle of summer isn't too late to imagine a singular upwards focus and direction in which your volcano of growth can burst forth.

One way to do this is to choose one word for the year to hone in on what you need to work on. You may have heard of this technique, and I highly recommend giving it a try.

In the book *My One Word*[2] author and Pastor Mike Ashcraft shares the benefits of picking one word for the year and viewing everything you do that year through that lens.

Here are just a few examples of words you could use:

1) Intentional

2) Surrender

3) Peace

4) Focus

5) Patience

6) Discipline

7) Courage

8) Strength

9) Freedom

10) Contentment

The word you choose is entirely up to you, but the idea is that through

2   Ashcraft, Mike, and Rachel Olsen. *My One Word: Change Your Life with Just One Word.* Zondervan, 2013.

prayer and careful consideration, you will choose the word that God puts on your heart. Even if you aren't spiritual, this exercise can still be highly useful. Pick the word that best represents where you want to grow and what you want to do this year.

If you want to spend more time with family, your one word might be "family." It's simple, but can you imagine the mind-blowing results of this focus if every major decision for a year is filtered through this lens? You will find yourself nurturing your closest relationships and spending more time with family, plain and simple.

If you love superheroes and want to be more heroic in real life, you could choose "heroic," or even make your one word the name of your favorite superhero.

(I wanted to make mine Iron Man, but it didn't fit quite right. There's always next year, right?)

Or you could get as creative as my wife and choose your word, and then find the Icelandic word to match. It's up to you how creative you want to get. Doesn't "hugrakkur" sound a lot cooler and more inspiring than just plain "brave?" I think so!

To start the thought process about your one word or point of focus for the year, ask yourself:

1) What do I want to accomplish in the upcoming year?

2) What kind of person do I want to become?

3) What do I want my focus to be as I move forward?

Answer these questions and you will start to have an idea of what your word should be.

Get all of your ideas out on paper. Once you have a list of potential words, here is how you narrow the list down:

- A friend or loved one picks the word which is their favorite for you.

- Pray continually to align your heart with God's heart for you.

- Cross off words that don't fit, and circle the best choices that represent one thing you want to change for the year.

- Once you have your list narrowed down to ten words, pick the best option of those ten.

- For more details on picking a word go to My One Word Here: http://myoneword.org/pick-your-word.

Now that you have your word, make sure it is visible for you every day by using it as your computer password, putting it on your bathroom mirror, or making a poster out of it. You can also use outside help to remind you of your word.

For example, my Life Group from church is currently practicing this exercise, and we are helping each other to walk through it. Over the course of this year we have constantly referred back to it, and it has made a huge difference in our lives.

I chose "steadfast" as my focus word beginning in 2018. I have a tendency to chase shiny objects, and my follow-through is lacking at times. I have become much better in this area as of late, and I know it's due to the increased focus on my one word.

I've found that being able to refer back to this word reminds me of my ultimate focus. It's hard to remember to direct every single decision through this lens, but when I do, it adds a higher level of clarity to any situation.

I now have the habit of asking, "Does this new task relate to my overall goals?" If it does, then great! If not, I need to seriously consider whether or not it's worth my time.

For me, focusing on being more consistent and following through means seeing things all the way to completion. I've found much personal and professional growth by keeping this at the forefront of my mind.

Your one word should be the word that will bring you the best possible results and will challenge you the most. Consider the word as your volcano's foundation for increased momentum.

Find a word that will best fit your goals or direction. You might be able to think of one right off the bat. If so, great! Write it down (with pen or paper or digitally) and put it somewhere you will see it every day.

Give yourself this quick win. You will find that your battle for momentum just got about 10x easier now that you have a point of reference and a new lens through which to view all of life's major decisions.

Focus up, fledgling volcano, as you start to heat up! We are going to be bursting forth in no time.

BUSTING THE NEUTRAL MYTH

"When you find yourself in the thickness of pursuing a goal or dream, stop only to rest. Momentum builds success."
—Suzy Kassem

"Life is like riding a bicycle. To keep your balance, you must keep moving."
—Albert Einstein

The first stop on our way to bursting forth with volcanic momentum is to recognize that we are pushing upwards or we are sinking down.

You are never neutral: you are going backwards or forwards. You are like a pendulum that never stops swinging. Your volcano of growth doesn't sit idle. It can't. It either recedes back into the earth or explodes upwards.

Whether it's an important relationship, weight loss goals, or your career, stagnation doesn't exist. It's either forward or backward, friend, there is no middle ground. You are either progressing or falling behind.

You can either get life or life will get you.

This concept is hard for some to crack, as stagnation can set in without even realizing it. Some goals are impossible to truly achieve because maintaining them is the goal.

I'm fairly average in quite a few things, so it has taken me years to figure out how to achieve lasting change. Just when I think I've arrived at a goal and I'm good to go, I slip. That describes my battle with weight loss most of my life.

I had recently finished the Whole30 healthy eating program and broke it by eating a cinnamon bun (and a s'mores cookie, but it looked so good you would have, too). As soon as I finished it, I wanted to go get another one. That slope is so slippery.

Like with all bad habits, my battle with healthy eating began with poor lifestyle choices. Three cans of mountain dew a day will not make a tubby kid less round. My college years were ripe with wonder and discovery, except that most of what I was discovering was that I loved Chinese food, I wouldn't immediately die from a sugar overdose, and that salads were nasty.

I ate about as well as you would expect of a college student who was off on his own, ten hours from his parents' home-cooked dinners. I am less than proud to admit that during my four years at college, I gained over fifty pounds.

Long story short, it took a doctor telling me to lose weight for me to get my head on straight and my pants size down.

I wrote a book about it that turned into my very own weight loss memoir. It's called *The Action Diet* and it's worth a read if you are looking to make small changes to live a healthier life. You can learn from my mistakes and avoid making similar ones.

It has been a long journey with trials and challenges but now I am in the best shape of my life. After I completed the Whole30 I felt great. I am now closer to my ideal weight than I have ever been.

That being said, I realized that there is never a point, with physical health at least, at which we have arrived. Right now I have more muscle and less fat than I've ever had. But the sad fact is that we are all in a state of decay and must fight to keep good health. Aging is an uphill battle.

If I hope to maintain my good health (which I do), I must keep working at it and stay ahead of the downward losing curve as much as possible. I must keep pushing upwards towards the surface.

This is also true for life a lot of times. You feel like you understand something, only to find out you really don't. Or you think you've arrived and completed a goal, and the journey is only getting started.

Life is a challenge and we must be vigilant if we are to stay on top of things, but too often we miss the mark. We take too long to realize we are trending downwards, and then life slams a door in our face while we're sitting on the couch eating potato chips.

This losing curve applies not only to weight loss and health, but any positive life direction we aim to take. If we aren't at least inching forward, we are crashing backwards.

Don't put effort into your marriage? It will decline and you and your spouse will grow apart.

Neglect investing time and effort in your kids early on? Good luck with them as teenagers.

If you don't work on your job skills you may become obsolete and soon find yourself expendable.

Name any skill in your arsenal. Unless it's riding a bike, chances are it will take time to get back into it if you don't practice.

Most of us spend our lives seeking comfort and protection, when adventure and challenge are often what spurs our greatest growth.

Think about this: If you put your car into neutral at any given place on the road, you will either start moving forward or backward. There are no perfectly flat roads on earth that will let you sit exactly where you are. If your aim is for neutral living, you eventually will crash.

Volcanic Momentum 101

"Without continual growth and progress, such words as improvement, achievement, and success have no meaning."

—Benjamin Franklin

Remaining neutral is not an option if we wish to grow. We all make mistakes and fall back from time to time. We are finite human beings who don't have time to do everything. Some things will falter as we pursue lofty goals and make our dreams come true.

The key, then, to growth explosion is to dive headfirst into the problem. You need to define what's stopping you and tackle that one thing. To do this, we will need to channel volcanic momentum. This approach involves identifying the next step in the process and stepping out in faith and confidence. It might hurt, but ultimately it will feel good to try something new.

You know the next step you should take, even if that step is to brainstorm your next step. Do something that will move you forward.

Don't hesitate. Take the leap and take that next step. It's almost always better to leap first and ask questions later, especially if you are normally hesitant to try new things.

What is the first step to take?

If you:

- Want to lose weight, what is the first thing you need to cut out from your life? (milkshakes, sodas, candy bars). What do you need to add to your life to make it better? (meditation, goal tracking, fitness).

- Want to bolster your marriage? Start with making your spouse a priority and schedule a date night with no kids, no phones, and no distractions.

- Want to quit your job? Make a plan to figure out what *you* need to do to make it happen. Don't make any drastic decisions, but plan the first steps towards a better future.

Everyone has a unique answer to this question, but you should be able to answer it if you look introspectively.

You might not have a firm idea how to get to the end of the goal, but I believe we all know the next step, even if that step is small. Take that next step today and don't accept the inevitable slide back.

Neutral myth busted. Read on for more goal-getting wisdom.

SAGS, BHAGS, AND DESTINY GOALS

"One way to keep momentum going is to have constantly greater goals."
—Michael Korda

For all sad words of tongue or pen, the saddest are these: 'It might have been!'"
—John Greenleaf Whittier

"Sag it up, baby."

Such was the Mantra of my book *Now What? Getting Unstuck in a Sticky World.*

Yah I know, you might be thinking, "Uhh what? This dude's cray..."

I am, but SAGs are not. Setting small goals is the start of major success. I firmly believe that the magma of life progress isn't gonna push itself to the surface unless you help it out a bit. Your goals won't complete themselves. Once you consider where you're going, you have to figure out how to make it happen. That's where SAGs, BHAGs, and Destiny Goals come in.

I break goals into three main categories, and I'd urge you to consider your top goal at each level:

- SAGS (Small Attainable Goals): These goals give you quick wins which are key to momentum and early growth. These get the magma flowing.

- BHAGS (Big Hairy Audacious Goals): BHAG is a concept first developed in the book *Built to Last*[3] by Jim Collins. Large goals that, once completed, leave a crater of impact on your life. These are bursts of magma flowing up to the surface.

- Destiny Goals: These are the goals that go beyond you. These are the goals that you want to achieve to leave a legacy. These completed goals blow up the entire mountain, changing the view of the landscape for now and generations to come.

You should have goals at all three levels. Start with SAGs and get your life going in the right direction. Then set and achieve BHAGs for explosive growth. Lastly, change the lives of others by setting Destiny Goals.

Having goals at all three levels will form the cornerstones of momentum. Growth will always come to a halt if we don't have a clear picture of what it is we are shooting for. Gaining momentum is only possible with goals.

Small Attainable Goals

Consider these goals as the base in your entire structure and progress. Volcanic Momentum cannot be achieved if you don't get some quick wins under your belt.

Here are some prime examples of a SAG:

- Losing five pounds
- Reading two books in one month
- Asking your boss for a raise

---

3   Collins, Jim, and Jerry I. Porras. *Built to Last: Successful Habits of Visionary Companies*. Harper Business, 2004.

- Writing 5,000 words in your novella
- Choosing a language-learning program and taking the beginners level course

These types of goals will light the fire towards even bigger and better goals.

I never would have built my fifth website if I hadn't built the first one. If I hadn't completed the SAG to get a crash course in website building from my brother-in-law, I never would have gotten to the point I am at now.

MarriageIsIntentional.com was the first website I put together. It was awful (and still is, go ahead and check it out, but visitor beware). The writing is bad, the content and images are ugly, and the formatting is all over the place. I also designed the logo myself. Enough said. It was just bad all around.

I look at that one compared to JMRing.com and I am still struck by the amount of progress. Now, I know I still have a long way to go to build truly inspiring and motivational content and websites, but I am so much further along now compared to where I started.

When I first set out to make my initial set of SAGs they were simple in nature. Write my first posts, get my website up, just start.

Starting (and most likely failing) is why SAGs are so important. You may not be able to accomplish them all the first time through. There's a high chance you will fail in at least a few. Now imagine failing on part of a bigger goal; it might have had you quitting.

If I had wanted to get 1,000 subscribers in my first year of building a platform I would have failed, but having small attainable goals brought me back to reality.

The point isn't to set your sights low. Not at all. As we will soon discuss, having big goals is of the utmost importance, but first you have to build up that pressure in your volcano.

Start with SAGs, get some quick wins, and then set your sights higher.

Big Hairy Audacious Goals

"A goal should scare you a little and excite you a lot."
　—Joe Vitale

These goals are the next tier after you start to achieve your SAGs. These are the personal goals you didn't really think you would ever achieve. They are not quite at the level of Destiny Goals, but are still huge and will take some time to complete.

These are the types of goals that don't seem possible at first, but they are attainable if worked at over time. For example:

- Reach your ideal weight and get washboard abs.
- Earn $10,000 a month in passive income to achieve the ultimate flexibility and spend more time with family and fully enjoy life.
- Save up for a ship that you can use to sail the world in one year.
- Go one month without watching TV to give more time to your family.
- Travel to Iceland and hike for seven days straight.
- Become a volleyball instructor and teach at a local high school.

BHAGs are not achievable overnight. You will need a consistent burst of momentum from completing SAGs in order to make these a reality.

Once you do achieve these, your life will change for the better.

When I was able to move into working online full time after three years of steady hustling on the side, I felt incredible. It was such a monumental achievement that would not have been possible without the consistent effort I put into SAGs.

Some personal examples of BHAGs

1) To pay off my student loans completely by the end of 2019.

2) To be location-independent and live and work in another country for three to six months.

3) To hit and maintain my ideal weight, and to continue to push myself physically with boot-camp workouts, long walks, and tennis and other sports.

BHAGs are the road to Destiny Goals. Don't skip over them in the aim to change the world. Achieve them and look ahead towards a bigger future.

As you will see, the main differentiator between BHAGs and Destiny Goals is that BHAGs are about your personal goals, and Destiny Goals also involve making a difference for others.

We have to first put on our own oxygen mask before we can help others. Grow yourself first, and then catapult yourself into your destiny.

Destiny Goals

Destiny Goals do not involve slaying a dragon and saving the princess, nor do they involve saving the world from giants or sailing the seven seas in search of hidden treasure.

Destiny Goals are the "big what" we seek in our everyday, fairly normal lives. I have come to grips with the fact that Hagrid isn't going to pick me up one day and bring me to Hogwarts, I'm not going to find a dragon's egg in the woods, nor am I going to discover a hidden force-power within. As much as I would love to have a fantastical destiny like the ones we read about in books or see in the movies, I know I'm destined for other things.

The truth is that these types of fantastical journeys are not possible for us, and it can make us feel like we won't ever amount to anything.

Compared to elite business moguls like Bill Gates or Elon Musk we might think that our own lives could never amount to anything. Our own SAGs and BHAGs may seem miniscule. What could we hope to accomplish that would come close?

On the road to making passive income one of my mentors has been Pat Flynn. He runs an extremely popular podcast called the *Smart Passive Income Podcast*. He shows others how he built up his own passive income and now has over $100,000 coming in every month passively.

I am nowhere near the monetary level of Pat Flynn, and yet I know my own progress has merit. I don't have anywhere near the following of Pat Flynn, but even if I help one person, isn't it worth it in the end?

Still, I often feel the weight of a goal that just isn't coming to fruition, and I feel hopeless, overwhelmed, and not good enough.

I am here to tell you this line of thinking is so utterly false I'd like to blow it up with a Death Star and kiss it goodbye forever (until a second one shows up, and a third… and probably a fourth). We each have inside of us a destiny that can change the world.

I believe God is working in all of us to pull that destiny out of us and lead us to our true potential. Remember that God wants us to get where God wants us to go, much more than we do, but if we don't work towards it, we won't ever get there.

We each have a destiny to seek and find. Actually, we each have several. If you have ever thought to yourself, "Yes! This is what I was born to do!" You might be pretty darn close to your destiny.

Destiny technically means something that is going to happen to you. That's a boring definition if you ask me. For me, destiny means God-given potential just waiting to be unleashed into the world at large.

But how do we ultimately find our destiny? By setting Destiny Goals, of course!

Destiny Goals take your thinking outside the box and get your mind thinking big.

What are Destiny Goals?

Before you start setting your own Destiny Goals, it's important to know what they entail and how they are formed. Remember that this is your direct link to discovering your true purpose. Destiny Goals have the following epic characteristics:

- Destiny Goals usually develop from the ground up and start as a SAG or a BHAG and might not be immediately clear.

- Outside the box in nature—think big!

- Contain the potential to change the world in real and lasting ways that will continue after you are gone; a lasting legacy.

- Inspiring to others.

- Will make a difference in the lives of others.

- A goal that can't be accomplished quickly and will need work put into it.

- Requires the help of others to complete it.

- Is something important to you.

- Has a creative and innovative element, as often the best solutions are the ones no one has yet considered.

- Is a direct upgrade from a SAG or a BHAG.

Only you can make the true distinction between a regular old BHAG and a superpowered and mighty Destiny Goal.

The important thing is that you are not limiting yourself or your potential with these goals. Sure, picking "I want to slay a dragon" would be ridiculous, but why not choose the real-world equivalent: get a doctorate in theology to empower individuals to seek God first, or discover a new way to stave off world hunger.

Destiny Goals can change the world by tapping into the potential of each of us as individuals to bring about bigger change. How you choose to change the world is entirely based on your own experiences and life circumstance. We are all on different life paths, but harnessing your uniqueness into the power of a Destiny Goal will give you firm and clear direction.

As noted earlier in this book, back in April 2015 Miranda and I set a big Destiny Goal to move away from Pennsylvania. We were out walking one day and we both immediately felt called to do more. We felt as if we were not accomplishing much with what we were doing at the time. We realized we needed to pray and seek out a big change.

We originally set a BHAG to be out of Pennsylvania by the end of the year. Having never made a huge move before as a couple, this would be a big deal. We had spent the last four years in the same apartment doing the same things.

Unbeknownst to us at the time, that BHAG was turning into a major Destiny Goal. God was working to change us big time. We prayed for a big change, dreamed for a challenge to work through, and boy did we get it! The journey turned out to be a huge learning curve and a major challenge for us both.

Throughout two years of working for three different retirement communities, we were stretched and pushed to our absolute limits. We rode an emotional roller coaster as the days faded together in a hazy blur.

I can't remember a time in my life where I have felt such a high level of joy, mixed with such a high level of stress. While the job stressed us out big time, it became the challenge we had prayed so dearly for. I wouldn't trade the time we spent there for anything. We were sharpened and strengthened as individuals and also as a couple.

The residents meant the absolute world to us and we miss them dearly still. Even though we may not have been able to articulate it at the time, our experience there was a Destiny Goal, because we could make a huge difference in the lives of many people.

This is the truth I've discovered about setting Destiny Goals and working towards crafting a legacy:

Setting Destiny Goals involves working and praying towards an unknown future. I may have no idea what my legacy is going to be (I don't!), but it doesn't mean I shouldn't work toward something.

Consider your purpose and greater destiny. What might your greater calling be? What positive change could you make on the world? How could you impact someone else's life in a significant and measured way?

Finding our purpose through our destiny comes from being able to push past doubt, pain, and fear. Do you think for a second that Miranda and I weren't frightened to leave our families behind and move 741 miles to an unknown future? Heck yeah, we were scared! But we didn't let that stop us, and it shouldn't stop you from dreaming about your future and the difference you can make.

We have one life. One short blip on this Earth. If you aren't dreaming into something, if you are just drifting along and hoping things will just fall into place… wake up, friend. Start dreaming now before your life passes you by and you are in the ground with a mound of dirt over your head.

Your Destiny Goals: Making the Impossible Possible!

"Most people overestimate what they can do in one year and underestimate what they can do in ten years."
 —Bill Gates

Now that you are pumped up to set Destiny Goals, keep in mind that your new enthusiasm won't last throughout the duration of the goal. I've found out the hard way that some days you just have to keep working towards the goal, even if you don't feel like it that day.

Albert Einstein said, *"Learn from yesterday, live for today, hope for tomorrow. The important thing is not to stop questioning."*

Discovering your destiny begins with asking yourself a few serious and pointed questions. It's painful at first, but gets easier over time. Questioning ourselves and the world is how we grow and find meaning. It's how we get to know ourselves truly.

If we can begin to question our beliefs, motives, goals, and the world around us, we will find our purpose and can move forward.

You will find true joy in becoming the person you were made to be, and it starts with pondering these questions:

1) If you could do absolutely anything in your life what would that be? Really get outside the box here and consider all options, whether or not it seems possible.

2) What in life brings you the most joy?

3) Who are the people you want to dream big with?

4) What are your unique passions and abilities?

5) How can you transform those passions and abilities into something that can make a difference in the world?

6) Bam, you're twenty years older… What do you most regret? What things do you wish you had done? (Fact: When interviewed later in life, people regret the things they didn't do[4] much more often than the things they did!)

7) Where do you want to go? The moon might be out of reach for most, but the world is open to us. If you have ever travelled, you know how good it can feel to experience new things. Even if the travel itself is stressful, it's great for growth.

Answering these questions isn't easy, but doing so will get your mind going. Answer these questions, ponder them, and then get ready for the final step in the process.

---

4   Bluerock, Grace. "The 9 Most Common Regrets People Have At The End Of Life." Mindbodygreen, Mindbodygreen, 2 Jan. 2016, www.mindbodygreen.com/0-23024/the-9-most-common-regrets-people-have-at-the-end-of-life.html.

Brainstorming Destiny Goals and Breaking the Box

"Your focus determines your reality"

    —Qui-Gon Jinn

Your ultimate purpose is the interplay between your passions and reality. It's the intersecting point between your abilities and your current circumstances and situation.

You can't truly understand the depths of poverty and homelessness unless you've either lived it or experienced it. You can't change the political atmosphere if you have no interest in politics, and you probably can't write a book if you don't know how to write.

We know all of this, and yet it is this exact thinking that stops us from dreaming big. We think, "I don't know how to speak Spanish so I could never travel to Ecuador." Or maybe "Even if I move to L.A. I will still never attain my dream of becoming an actress; I'm not pretty enough."

This limited thinking is detrimental to positive and productive brainstorming sessions. Break outside of the box and create big goals by limiting these thoughts. Believe that *anything* is possible!

The best way to get started?

Have a Destiny Goal Brainstorming Session.

Take the following steps to discover your Destiny Goals:

1) Grab a friend, family member, or significant other. Make sure they are on board with the process and are willing to stretch your thinking.

2) Get a sheet of paper, a journal, or a laptop to take notes.

3) Find a place to sit that won't distract you.

4) **Ponder the questions listed above,** but focus mainly on #1 (what would you do with your life if nothing at all was holding you back?). Don't limit your thinking and don't be afraid to be "ridiculous."

5) Shoot ideas back and forth with your brainstorming partner and write everything down. Fill up a page with things you would like to do with your life. Use the person with you to bounce ideas off you and to keep you thinking big. When we did this, Miranda had to keep telling me to get outside of the box! I was stuck in a mindset of possible.

6) Don't let this activity become a one-time thing. Post your goals onto a whiteboard, or keep the notes next to your bed. Add to it whenever you think of something big you want to accomplish.

As a reminder: I've created a rad list of 100 Destiny Goals as part of the companion guide for this book. You can download it here: www.JMRing.com/volcanic-momentum-bonuses.

Where you put your efforts and determination is where you will start to see your dreams become reality. If you spend time focusing on your Destiny Goals, your reality will soon follow. You will start to sleep, dream, and eat your goals.

Your focus determines your reality. Be a self-fulfilling prophecy.

Momentum will only come when you have a clear direction for what you are doing. Master the art of goal setting with the three levels of goals and you will be well on your way to bursting from point A all the way to point Z.

Not even the Road Runner will escape your quick feet.

Examples of SAGs, BHAGs, and Destiny Goals

Here some examples of how the three main types of goals can be constructed, but remember that Destiny Goals are the big kahunas. They are what we are striving towards.

Personal Health:

1) SAG: Lose five pounds over the next two weeks

2) BHAG: Hit my ideal weight in the next three months through good eating and lots of exercise

3) Destiny Goal: Create a national fitness franchise that pairs with motivational stars like Jillian Michaels to transform the lives of people who previously had no access to conventional exercise resources

Learning a New Language:

1) SAG: Enroll in or download a language-learning app

2) BHAG: Hold a conversation with a fluent speaker in the language

3) Destiny Goal: Use my new skill to translate for a group on a missions trip

Gaining Knowledge:

1) SAG: Read two books this week

2) BHAG: Read fifty books in one year

3) Destiny Goal: Give away each of the print books you acquired to a local library that partners with schools to provide books to those that need them most.

Goals Action Step

Now that you have started to think about goals, it's time to write down some of your own!

Take this process at your own pace, but don't rush. You will see as you continue to read that much of the journey is about the small wins and small changes.

Write down your answers to these three questions:

1) What is one small thing I want to accomplish right away? (SAG)

2) What's a bigger personal goal I have that I can accomplish this month? (BHAG)

3) How can I use my current skills and goal progress to help another person? (Destiny Goal)

READY, SET, TRACK!

"Setting goals is the first step in turning the invisible into the visible."

—Tony Robbins

If you don't know where you're going, how will you know when you've arrived?

That's a simple question really, but if you aren't clear about what you are shooting for, you might end up drifting along with nothing to grab onto.

Now that you have been introduced to the three different types of goals, it's time to set your own, and decide on a way to track those goals. Pull out your list now, as you will need it for this chapter. (You did write down some goals, right? Oh, you already have your goals list ready to go? Wow, you are one step ahead!)

We are going to talk about the final piece to setting up a firm foundation to reach your goals: tracking!

Tracking is fun, and I've found it's often more fun than even doing the goal itself. The purpose of tracking is to find a way that works for you to show you where you've been, where you're at, and where you want to go.

Tracking can be done in many different and variably creative ways, but here are four that I recommend:

1) Whiteboards (or some sort of display)

My wife and I are obsessed with whiteboards. Just ask any of our friends. When they visit our apartment they see mostly blank white walls until we hear… "Hey guys, what's this?"

We say, "Oh yeah. That's just one of our goal boards…"

To this day we still get embarrassed by this conversation. I don't know why, because having goals is pretty awesome, but we get awkward about our weirdness. It would be so much easier if everyone else displayed their Destiny Goals for all to see!

Still, weird or not, whiteboards allow you to have a real life visual in front of you to see progress. We have not found a better way to keep track of where we have been, where we are, and where we are going.

Your display doesn't have to be a whiteboard, but it should be visible somewhere every day, and changeable as needed. Make the display your own, but have a good mix between SAGs, BHAGs, and Destiny Goals.

Capture memories through goal progress instead of filling your wall with cutesie pictures of cats.

2) Goal Journal

"Good habits are hard to form and easy to live with. Bad habits are easy to form and hard to live with. Pay attention. Be aware. If we don't consciously form good ones, we will unconsciously form bad ones."

—Mark Matteson[5]

One common theme in almost all self-help books seems to be

---

5   Matteson, Mark. *Freedom from Fear: The Story of One Man's Discovery of Simple Truths That Lead to Wealth, Joy and Peace of Mind.* Ugly Dog Publishing, 2002.

journaling. I read again and again advice from bestselling authors and thought leaders who recommend keeping a journal. It's one of the best habits we can form.

Mark Matteson, in his book *Freedom from Fear*, recommends keeping a journal with you at all times to keep up momentum and progress towards good habits. It was his recommendation that broke me down and convinced me that I needed to start journaling on the regular.

Journaling is not only good for the soul, it's also fantastic for tracking goals. Especially if it's a journal you keep with you at all times, you can constantly update it as you start to accumulate and accomplish goals.

Writing goals down is just one more step to making things happen and getting stuff done. Give yourself the wins that come with accomplishing goals by dedicating a standalone journal to tracking your goals. This way can get messy to organize, and won't work for everybody, but for some it can be the best way to track progress.

If you find yourself in between the digital world and the real world when it comes to notes and organization, consider giving Rocketbooks a try.

Rocketbooks are journals with a twist. You can write in them, quickly upload the contents to an online storage that you designate using the Rocketbook app, and then erase the book with a wet cloth to keep it fresh. You can do this an almost unlimited number of times.

By using a Rocketbook I have been journaling more. I keep the small notebook with me wherever I go. I don't have to worry about losing my content or running out of space. It's the perfect solution to journaling that fits my lifestyle.

I'd give it a try if you are looking for a hip and easy way to journal on the regular.

3) Good ol' Fashioned Spreadsheet

I love spreadsheets. I have far too many. But what's one more, right?

One of my favorite sheets is called my "level 50 life spreadsheet" a term which comes from the book *Level Up Your Life*[6] By Steve Kamb.

I've broken up all of my life's goals into different sections with an eye to put a finish date on the ones that I have accomplished.

This way I have a broad scope of my goals and can see what I'm working toward, but I can also see where I've been. I can see that there is a lot that I have left to do, but also a lot that I have already accomplished.

It's a great way for us tech-savvy folks who are always sitting at our computer to have our goals right in front of us.

4) The Seinfeld Method: Don't Break the Chain

You may have heard of this one, but it's great for building habits and tracking singular goals.

Each day that Jerry Seinfeld wrote and practiced his jokes, he would put a big red X on a calendar. His only goal? To not break the chain. He would do his very best to work every day towards his dream of being a comedian by not missing a day.

If you have a singular focus and one main goal you are working towards, this method for tracking will work towards building a strong habit.

---

6   Kamb, Steve. *Level up Your Life: How to Unlock Adventure and Happiness by Becoming the Hero of Your Own Story.* Rodale Books, 2016.

Goal Tracking Final Thoughts

For more on goal tracking, I recommend reading the book I referenced above (*Level Up Your Life* by Steve Kamb). The book showed me how much fun (and important) it is to track goals and inspired me to reach the next level.

In the book, Steve shares fun ways to track goal progress by turning it into a game. This approach is next level in theory, but is so much fun to put into practice. I recommend checking it out if you are particularly stuck on how to track goals, or just find the process mind-numbingly boring. (Side note: the hardcover is in full color which is super cool.)

You can use a combination of whiteboards, physical journals, spreadsheets, the Seinfeld Method, a Rocketbook, or a myriad of apps or other creative ways to track goals. The goal-tracking medium is far less important than actually tracking the goal.

Figure out where you want to go, what you want to do, and who you want to be, and then write down your ideas. Get your head out of the box and let your creative side flourish.

Set up your tracking and get ready for some serious momentum like you've never had before!

Section Two:
9 STRATEGIES TO MASTER YOUR MOMENTUM

Strategy #1:
MASTERING THE ENERGY CODE

*"Momentum is not the result of one push,
it's the result of many continual pushes over time"*

—John C. Maxwell[7]

It's inevitable. At some point when reaching for a big dream we lose energy. Often this is one of the first killers of momentum, and as such, we must learn to master our energy levels first. You can't finish out goals without energy.

Life always comes along and pits us against a rock and a hard place. If we aren't prepared to fight for our energy conservation, our motivation to complete goals will disappear when we least expect it, and it will be hard to recover.

Eventually our bodies scream at us in a high-pitched whine "I need energy!" and we may have one or more of the following thoughts:

- I can't even write one more page in my book…
- I just can't eat one more piece of broccoli…
- Get that study guide OUT OF MY FACE!
- *Ahh!*

---

7   Maxwell, John C. *No Limits: Blow the CAP off Your Capacity.* Center St., 2017.

What are we to do about our lack of energy? How do we solve this puzzle on a consistent and ongoing basis that doesn't rely on energy drinks and month-long vacations?

Enter **"The Energy Code,"** the secret to mastering the basics of energy creation and conservation that will have you blasting towards your goals.

I don't know about you, but when I am working towards a bigger goal I always hit the so-called "slump," and my energy dips way down. I find myself in a rut and I don't want to keep going.

The end goal seems too far away, and the progress I've already made doesn't seem to be worth the frustration.

Volcanic Momentum depends on high energy levels and we should prepare ourselves to fight this battle against fatigue.

We must recognize the inevitable loss of energy and plan to strike back before it's too late.

The following are **ten ways you can maintain high energy levels**. I recommend mastering them before the slump takes hold. Better yet, position yourself to always be formulating positive habits.

We need to learn our personal "energy code" unique to each of us. Find a combination of the tips below to create plentiful energy for your specific needs.

For endless energy, ditch the Red Bull and dive in here.

I Need Energy Right NOW! Energy Code Level 1: Start with the Basics. Eat Healthy

As of this writing my wife and I recently completed the Whole30 eating program. In it, we ate only veggies, meat, fruits, and nuts for thirty days. Most common convenience foods are off limits.

It's designed to give your body a break from foods that can wreak havoc in your digestive and immune systems, like dairy and gluten, and to give you a chance to figure out what foods might cause a problem. This diet is simple in design, and a very good way to reset your system.

Even though I do love how eating healthy makes me feel, it's still difficult to do in practice and has taken a lot of work. It's worth it though, because when I eat well I have a ton of energy and feel great.

You need not do the Whole30 to get sustainable energy. All you need to do is eat healthier and make better choices. Sugar might give you a quick boost of energy, but over time your body will not respond well.

Grabbing a Starbucks specialty coffee once in a while? Sure, go for it! If you are a writer, studying hard for an exam, or need a boost to finish a very important deliverable for a client, then by all means grab a cup. Treat yourself occasionally, just don't make it an everyday thing.

It's important to strike a balance. There are parts of doing something like the Whole30 that can seem more exhausting than it's worth! Shopping and cooking all of your own meals can tire even the most energetic person. But I learned from the process, and that knowledge is priceless.

Strike a balance and enjoy food, but also consider what you are putting into your body. Our main source of energy starts with the foods we eat, so learn to be mindful of your eating decisions.

Since this book isn't a weight loss guide, we won't delve into the details of healthy eating, but I do encourage you to question your eating habits and ask "Is this the best I can do?" Are there any eating habits you could change that would make a huge difference in your energy levels, and your life?

Start with the absolute basics and give your body the energy it needs for the long-haul.

Three Quick Win Ideas:

1) Pack an apple in your bag instead of a candy bar.
2) Drink a full glass of water before every meal.
3) Make a healthy trail mix to take on your commute in place of coffee.

I Still Need Energy: Energy Code Level 2: Get enough Sleep

"Think in the morning. Act in the noon. Eat in the evening. Sleep in the night."

— William Blake

I have to write this one here. We all know this to be true, but how often is sleep the FIRST thing we give up when trying to create more time?

Answer: It's always the first thing.

According to a CDC study[8], one in three adults don't get enough sleep.

---

8 "CDC Press Releases." 1 In 3 Adults Don't Get Enough Sleep, 1 Jan. 2016, https://www.cdc.gov/media/releases/2016/p0215-enough-sleep.html.

We won't give up TV, family time, sporting events, the early-morning hustle, or even reading. Pretty much everything comes before sleep when setting our priorities and managing our time.

I recognize that parents, especially new parents, don't have the luxury of getting enough sleep on the regular. This certainly isn't the only example of sleep deprivation but it's the most common. However, most of us can find ways to prioritize sleep. You might think you can run off of less (and some people need less), but in reality you probably need seven to eight hours every night.

Many entrepreneurs and high achievers in particular fall prey to lack of sleep. If you take the advice from authors like Gary Vee (who I really like and respect), the result is either staying up until two or three and "bleeding from your eyeballs," as he would say, or getting up at five a.m. to hustle before work.

This can be good in the short term, as new entrepreneurs can find success through the hustle. My caution is that this shouldn't be your norm. If you have a side project to work on, don't make sleep the sacrifice to get it done.

If you feel like you get enough sleep at night but you don't go to bed until one a.m., are you groggy? Is your sleep schedule working for you?

If you do your best work in the morning, get up at five a.m. but go to bed earlier. If you do your best work at night, plan to sleep in the next day (if you can). Don't sacrifice sleep and your health to get to your dream more quickly. Be in it for the long haul.

Do your best to get enough sleep and fight to maintain a regular sleeping schedule. Your energy levels will thank you for it, and you will have enough momentum to finish your goals. Without sleep, it's not possible to finish strong. Do yourself a favor and get to bed on time.

Three Quick Win Ideas:

Make your sleep a priority by scheduling for it, not around it.

Make your bedroom a haven for sleep by getting rid of excess light coming from a window, TVs, and other distractions.

Practice deep breathing and stretching before bed.

My Energy is increasing: Energy Code Level 3: Stay Digitally Organized

Nothing kills energy more than not knowing what you are working on the next day, losing online documents, or not even remembering where you keep your passwords document. If you're like me, you hate when you:

- Can't find a standard document that your client is asking for.
- Need to enter data in multiple places and keep ten tabs open in order to have everything ready to copy-paste (job hunting for example).
- Feel overwhelmed by too many documents and spreadsheets.
- Think you are forgetting something really important…

One way to stay organized in a busy online world? Enter Trello, the world's most ridiculously simple project management tool. It will keep you organized and keep everything in one easy-to-remember place.

To see Trello in action, check out my YouTube page for a video of how I managed a book launch with Trello. You might also consider enrolling in my course on Trello for a guided walkthrough: www.JMRing.com/learn-trello.

Once you get used to saving your ideas, documents, must-do tasks, and your digital life in one easy-to-access place, you will feel a burden lift. Knowing I have everything I need in one place makes multiple projects easier to manage.

Beyond project management tools like Trello, focus on getting your digital life in order. Reduce online clutter to help you keep moving towards your goals.

Three quick win ideas:

1) Organize your desktop on your computer. Break it down to the smallest number of base folders possible.

2) Find a project management or to-do list program that you love, and make it the funnel for everything you do.

3) Make a habit out of cleaning the main idea funnel frequently, which will give you space to breathe and add new ideas.

Feeling Slightly More Energized: Energy Code Level 4: Get Organized in Real Life.

You would be amazed at the amount of energy that is drained by looking around at a messy room.

At the office, four hours are lost every week[9] due to clutter and lost paper. Is it even worth mentioning how much time you waste each and every day looking for things around the house?

---

9 Noria Corporation. Reduce Office Clutter to Increase Productivity, Efficiency and Profitability. 23 Mar. 2009, https://www.reliableplant.com/Read/16652/reduce-office-clutter-to-increase-productivity,-efficiency-profitability.

"Honey, where's my…"

Since my wife is an organizational guru, and a little bit of a nut when it comes to the removal of clutter, our home is pretty clear. It's not often that things go missing and for that I am thankful.

But it wasn't always that way. Nope! We look back at old pictures and see how much stuff we had strewn about everywhere, and I wonder how we ever got anything done. I see a direct correlation between our organization and the high volume of work we are able to consistently put out.

Being organized in the real world makes a huge difference in productivity levels as well as energy and is a small but critical part of the energy code. If you can quickly get to work every day on the important stuff and save your energy for those things, you will find success.

Don't waste time and energy living a disorganized life. Live a life free of clutter and new possibilities will open before you.

For more on getting organized in real life, you can see Miranda's course here: www.JMRing.com/declutter-course.

Three Quick Win Ideas:

1) Pick one room in your house and take everything out of it. Start fresh and only put back what is truly needed for that room to function.

2) Clear your desk of all unnecessary items.

3) Start to find a place for things to go once you are done with them. Eventually, each item in your house will have its place. This makes for ease of living and lends more energy to your most important tasks instead of chores.

I am Feeling Alive Again: Energy Code Level 5: Trim the Fat and Cut Out Unnecessary Tasks

We've all taken on more than we can handle at times. Life can get overwhelming fast, and before we know it time is flying by and we can't seem to get anything important done or spend quality time with those we love.

One of my favorite movie lines is spoken by the character Sadness in Pixar's *Inside Out*: *"Crying helps me slow down and obsess over the weight of life's problems."*

While it makes me chuckle, you probably don't want to be like Sadness and obsess over the weight of life's problems. Rather, take a hot minute, zoom out, and make a plan to break the pattern of overwhelm.

What's one way to pierce the fog that busyness creates and get a clear picture of our daily goings-on? Brainstorming.

Get a bird's-eye view of everything you do with a brain dump or a mind map. Find out what's going on at the big-picture level. What is taking up most of your time? What is sucking the energy out of you that should go to other tasks?

Here's an even scarier question: What is being neglected in your life?

Once you have a clearer big picture it's much easier to home in and decide what life responsibilities have to stay, and what can be cut. If you are pouring energy into the wrong things it will be that much harder to manage life's chaos.

Pull back on your overwhelming responsibilities. Chances are there are a few things that might need to go in order for you to dedicate the necessary time to reaching the right goals.

Wait! is this possible!?

It won't happen overnight, but yes, you can limit your obligations by learning to say no to the events and tasks that don't directly relate to your goals.

Don't go overboard with this. Go to Thanksgiving at your mom's house, play video games with friends once in a while, and by all means go play laser tag.

But know in your heart of hearts that it's okay to say "no," even if you feel you *should* do something. Make your choices based on your priorities and become more aware of what you are spending your time doing. Sometimes life is jammed in fifth gear and we barely have the energy to pull back, but saying no can be the life raft you've been looking for.

Say no to new "stuff" more often than you say yes. Especially start saying no more than yes if you find yourself busy just for busy's sake.

We will go more into saying no and mastering priorities as a method of creating time in a later chapter, but get a jump start by learning to say no more regularly. Remember the point is not to become a "no man" or a "never lady." Not at all. But unless you create time, you will never have the energy needed to finish your big and lofty Destiny Goals.

Three quick win ideas:

1) Say no to volunteering this weekend.

2) Say no to the next person that asks for your time.

3) Say no to your desire to keep working and grab a book instead.

I think I have Energy Now? Maybe? Energy Code Level 6: Line up Goals with Your Core Values (Hint: Remember those Destiny Goals?)

"When you are enthusiastic about what you do, you feel this positive energy. It's very simple."

—Paulo Coelho

I looked at my screen with wonder. "How to make 10k per month for the rest of your life" was the email subject line. I clicked. I read. I was hooked. Now I had a new plan. I would sell physical products through Amazon FBA (fulfillment by Amazon).

This was how I would make money online. This was how I was going to get my breakthrough! YES!

I spent weeks researching, taking courses, reading articles, and otherwise planning my foray into this world.

Then I hesitated.

I didn't act on what I learned. Maybe it would have been a great idea, but I realized before I even started that Amazon FBA had nothing to do with my core values, didn't relate to my other goals, and I would never enjoy it. So why was I going to do it?

I didn't have a good answer, so I changed plans. I'm so glad that I did. I could be knee deep in random items, boxes, and duct tape right about now!

I've since gotten better at stopping this derailed train before it starts, but I have a deep-rooted tendency to chase shiny objects. I love the new and exciting, often only because it's new and exciting.

The way I'm learning to get better at this is simple: I remember my core values and my Destiny Goals.

The next time you're tempted by a shiny new idea, ask yourself: How much does it relate to your current goals and tasks? If it directly relates (i.e., helping someone with book marketing will also help you get better at marketing your own books), then you're good.

If the new idea indirectly relates, it might be worth pursuing, but strongly consider the time-suck of learning the ins and outs of a new venture.

If you find that it doesn't relate at all, table it as a good idea for later on and keep working on your current tasks.

The best example I have for this is my dream to write a novel. I'd love to be a full-time fiction author. However, fiction would be a huge stretch for me because it's a different type of writing than I do now. It doesn't make sense right now. Eventually I will delve into this dream, but for now I will continue to work on my foundation so that one day I can take the risk and go for it.

My Destiny Goal of one day writing a bestselling and transformative novel is currently shelved until the timing is right.

Not all good ideas are necessarily good ideas *right now*. What shiny objects are getting in your way right now?

Again, this takes time to figure out and isn't easy by any means. You first need to nail down your core values and what you love doing and then compare these with what you spend your time doing.

For example, if your core values are family time, creative growth, and spiritual connection, then your goal needs to involve these things.

If your BHAGs are to spend time travelling and learn a new language, you can meet these goals as long as you bring your family along with you on your travels. But if you're away from family for months, not getting to spend time in creative mode, or your spiritual connection is waning from lack of attention, rethink your current goals or the way you are completing them.

Once your daily tasks intersect with your greatest desires, your energy levels will soar higher than you ever expected possible. Marry your output to what you were born to do, and reaching the goal just got a billion times easier.

Too many people spend far too much energy reaching for goals they don't even want. Make sure you actually want the goals you are pursuing! This seems simple, but double check that you are heading in the desired direction:

1) Figure out your core values and what you care about most.

2) Determine your Destiny Goals and match them with your core values.

3) Watch your inner energy reserves hum with increased vitality.

Your goal will come to pass in no time if you are aligned in this way.

Three quick win ideas:

1) Write down one of your core values and throughout the day think about how you can use that value to invest in others' lives.

2) Dedicate time every day towards working on just one of your biggest priorities.

3) Think about the daily activities that are on the fringe of your core values and don't relate to your goals. Could you do without these activities? We only have so much time available to us, we best make sure we aren't wasting it.

I Do Feel Better! Energy Code Level 7: Change Course as Needed to Avoid Burnout

I am a huge advocate of being real with yourself and your goals. Sometimes you just can't work towards certain goals anymore, at least for a while. For whatever reason, doing the one thing you know you should becomes impossible in the moment.

Sometimes I wake up and I just cannot do the work I know I need to do. I can't even will myself to sit down at my computer!

This is when I know burnout is starting to set in and I need a break, or I need to have a goal check-in to make sure I'm working toward the right things.

Be careful not to use this lack of energy as a cop out, but be real with yourself. If your goal to travel to eight countries in eight months is no longer workable or you fall behind due to life circumstances, change your goal.

Shoot for four countries instead of eight. Drive to Canada or Mexico and count that. Don't let your goals constrict you. You own your goals; they don't own you.

Goals should always be moldable and subject to change at any point. Crush your goals by believing in yourself, but don't get crushed in the process. Life happens. Hardship comes along in many forms. I don't have to give you examples of how life can knock you down. You know. We all know.

Work hard, but plan to change plans. When life happens, shift your plans and strike forth from a point of strength when you recover.

Three quick win ideas:

1) Take more breaks than you think you need, but then come back from a position of renewed energy.

2) Be real always. Don't force yourself to complete a goal just for the sake of completion.

3) Ask for help if needed, and always be open and willing to change course if roadblocks get in the way.

Getting Really Close Now! Energy Code Level 8: Do Something New and Exciting

A change of pace or something new can ignite lost energy levels. If you are feeling *blech* toward working on your goals, stop and try something new. You could:

- Rent a kayak and float down a lazy river.

- Play laser tag (can you tell I really want to go to laser tag?).

- Go to the movies alone. Trust me, you will feel so awkward your nerve endings will be on fire with new energy.

- Plan a trip to a brand-new country and actually go.

- Go to a brand-new restaurant.

- Pay for a coffee for the person behind you. This will light up your nerves and feed you more energy than you would expect, especially if the lady behind you says okay but then buys her own food, and doesn't actually say thank you (it happened).

We all know the rush we feel from going to a new place or trying something new. Sometimes this might just be all we need to take the next step towards a big goal.

It may seem like a simple thing to try some of the above, but energy comes when we actually do something new. Every time you take a risk and try something you've never done before, your brain physically grows and gets stronger, just like a muscle.[10] Learning to challenge yourself in this way will lead to abundant levels of energy as your brain adapts to these new experiences.

New experiences are your ticket to advancing one step closer to goal completion, massive amounts of energy, and a fulfilling life.

Three quick win ideas:

1) Go somewhere new today. Don't wait; go now!

2) Send a family member a nice card. It's always nice to receive something in the mail, isn't it? You will also feel good for sending it, so win-win.

3) Read a new book in a genre you aren't used to. It's good to step outside of your comfort zone once in awhile.

---

10   You Can Grow Your Intelligence. https://www.nais.org/magazine/independent-school/winter-2008/you-can-grow-your-intelligence/.

It's Becoming a Habit: Energy Code Level 9: Develop the Habit of Working Towards Your Goal Every Day, Even for Just Fifteen Minutes.

There is nothing better for positive momentum than forming the habit of working on your goal every single day. Even if it means forcing yourself to go on a short walk, writing for fifteen minutes, or writing a handwritten note to your mother to move towards your relationship goals. The tiny amount of extra work is all worth it in order to build momentum.

Starting is often the hardest part of habit formation and goal progress. If you can learn to work on your goal every single day (even if the progress is miniscule), it's still progress! Progress of any kind will give you sustained energy to meet your goals, and sometimes this is all we need to keep moving forward.

Habits are a huge topic among many self-help authors and gurus. I love reading about habit formation and the practice of reducing negative habits to pave the way for positive ones. But true habit expert I am not. Consider reading books from authors Michal Stawicki, Steve Scott, or Patrik Edblad for a far more in-depth discussion on habits. These authors dive in and show you how you can start forming positive habits fast and give you practical tips to get your habits on track.

Three quick win ideas:

1) Pick one new positive habit and work hard towards it now for at least seven days. Once you get to seven days, make it to thirty days to get the habit to stick.

2) Set up a calendar notification to go off every day, or find an app to remind you to complete that habit every day.

3) Keep up the habit chain with the Seinfeld method to develop your new skill.

Ponder and Reflect: Energy Code Level 10: Meditate on Your Goals

I meditate every single night before bed. I've been doing this for over a year now, and I can tell you it's made a huge difference in my life. Not only does it help to calm my system, enabling me to get a solid night's rest, it also helps to direct my thoughts in clearer ways.

If I meditate and allow myself to reach a center of cohesive thought, the effects are incredible. As my mind clears I see paths that didn't exist before, leading much more easily to goal completion. It takes time to reach this clarity, as my mind is usually all over the place, but the fluidity of thought that comes from sitting quietly is incredible.

Meditation allows your thoughts to manifest towards your goals, and what you need to get done in order to complete those goals. It helps your mind get in sync with the natural flow of the world around you, instead of the jumble of confusing thoughts and emotions that normally plague us.

This world is busy. I get caught up in that busyness as much as the next guy. When life seems to be running at a frantic pace, consider stopping to meditate and reflect upon your goals. Be honest with your thoughts and feelings, and learn to let go of negative emotions.

As a Christian with a faith in God, I find that putting myself in a posture of surrender is a good strategy. I lift my hands palm upwards and give up my worries and fears to Him, while also recognizing that I am called to do a good work and take action.

We can lean on God when our own strength feels insufficient, but we then have to work. If we get kicked down, we can't stay down.

Three quick win ideas:

1) Meditate every day for a set amount of time, no matter how short.

2) Reflect on where you have been and appreciate your success, achievement, and positive memories.

3) Imagine a future you having already completed your wildest Destiny Goal.

Final Thoughts on Mastering the Energy Code

Mastering the energy code and leveling up your goal-crushing abilities starts with these strategies. You can't become a master at momentum if you don't first learn to create and harness energy in all forms.

Go forth with a renewed mind and attack your goals with abandon. Promise yourself that you won't be too hard on yourself during the inevitable slump, and surge ahead when your energy returns.

Good luck my friend; may you be filled with boundless energy to change the world.

Strategy #2:
EMBRACING THE TORTOISE INSIDE OF YOU

*"Everything worthwhile in life—everything you want,
everything you desire to achieve, everything you want
to achieve—is uphill."*

—John C. Maxwell

It's hard to change. Even now that you have boundless energy, you still have to want to change and reach for something bigger than you are used to.

But the smallest changes in routine can mess with our minds. Even the most carefree among us struggles at times to adapt to change. Minor changes like waking up at a new time on Wednesdays, changing your morning commute because of a detour, or your doctor forcing you to switch to decaf coffee, can be a nuisance.

And let's not even start with life's other trials and derailed plans. Life is hard enough when things are going right; how can we even begin to think about working towards a goal when things are going poorly?

At heart, most of us are creatures of comfort, even if we like to tell ourselves we like change. Miranda and I would be the first to say we love change, until we are forced to admit we've watched through all nine seasons of *The Office* over five times!

The best advice here with making changes to work towards your goals? Start small.

Remember again the fact that we are never staying neutral. We are always going forward or backward. You will eventually need to master the art of moving forward in spite of life's tough circumstances.

The good news here is that small changes are easy to incorporate and keep the needle moving forward. Better yet, these small changes don't bring too much pain into the equation.

Big changes are something most of us hope to avoid forever. Our brains love knowing what's next, and uncertainty can drain energy as we focus on what could be and what we have to do to get there. If we start with small changes and challenge our immunity to change, life will never trample us. The only way to counter life's troubles is to learn how to face change with our heads up and backs straight.

Become like the tortoise and finish the race. It might not be pretty, but you can start now to get closer to the finish line, instead of getting lapped over and over again.

We strive for comfort, but it's really change that gets us to where we want to go.

I'd like to share five benefits to starting out with small changes and learning to live for delayed gratification:

1) It can be hard (and understandably so!) to feel inclined to make any change. Small life changes give you the quick win that you need to get started, without forcing you to face an insurmountable challenge.

2) Skip the overwhelm feeling that often comes with starting a new task. Take it easy, slowly working your way towards a new

future. Don't get stuck feeling like you are taking on too much at once. Get your small victories in to gain confidence.

3) Small goals are easier to complete and take less time. It will be hard NOT to want to make a small change, especially when you know you can accomplish it in just a few minutes.

4) You will feel great. Completing any goal, even a small one, feels amazing. Knowing you have moved one step closer to your bigger life goals is one way to make your day a success.

5) Small wins add up, and eventually culminate into bigger changes and bigger goal completion. Progress will grow exponentially; before long you won't even recognize the new you.

No one has the capacity to fully realize a Destiny Goal in a short period of time. It will take continuous minute changes to reach your bigger goals.

You can, however, reach your SAGs in no time if you commit to making small changes in your life. Goals are change incarnate. Once you start to SAG it up you can go after those BHAGs and then conquer your Destiny Goals.

Sure, there are people out there that can drop everything and lose 100 pounds and run a marathon in a month's time, but this is far from the norm, nor do I believe this approach will lead to lasting change.

Get some SAGs crossed off your goals list and make small changes for massive results. Become like the snail from *Kung Fu Panda*.

Wait… there wasn't a snail?!

There was, believe me, he was just too busy crushing life elsewhere to worry about Tai Lung and the dragon warrior.

To master the art of small changes use this simple three-step formula and discover small wins to get that momentum started:

1) Write a list of ten things you want to see improvement in, or say it out loud to yourself right now. Better yet, grab your list of SAGs from the previous chapter. You made that list, right?

2) Take one of your goals and make a plan to achieve that first step today (because you won't want to do it tomorrow).

3) Complete that one small step before you lose the energy required. Give yourself a quick win and revel in the feeling of moving one step closer to your goal.

Small changes need to be wins specific to you, and not necessarily wins for someone else.

Losing five pounds, showing up to work on time for a week straight, or writing up a one-pager for a business idea to send out to a few friends might be your next steps.

It doesn't matter what *your* next steps are, only that *you* take them.

Small changes are more attainable and as such will blast your momentum meter to level fifty.

Get your momentum to the highest possible level by giving yourself small wins all along the way. Consider making Destiny Goals and reaching for BHAGs of course, but don't underestimate the value of the small win when you are taking those courageous first steps.

Pretty soon you will be a goal crusher, and you will feel the power of unleashed fire and fury in your veins.

Hop to it. Before you move on to the next chapter, attain one of your SAGs.

Strategy #3:

THE #1 ENEMY OF MOMENTUM: WASTED TIME AND HOW TO AVOID IT

"The proper function of man is to live, not to exist. I shall not waste my days in trying to prolong them. I shall use my time."

—Jack London

Nothing stops you in your tracks like the feeling you are spinning your wheels and wasting time. Sometimes wasted time is the result of boredom, but most often it's the result of a lack of clear direction.

We have all faced these thoughts at one time or another:

"I don't feel like working. Let's do something fun!"

"I am so bored. What can I to do entertain myself?"

"I just don't feel like doing anything."

The truth is that time is precious and if we waste it trying to chase down entertainment, we will look back and regret our wasted time. The truth is, we can be wasting time even in the midst of our busyness.

Busyness is often the antivenom used to counter an increasingly dull and meaningless life. I've done it and I know firsthand that it's much easier to tack on a lot of "fun" activities to my plate rather than get my act together and figure out my purpose.

Henry David Thoreau said the following:

"It is not enough to be busy. So are the ants. The question is: What are we busy about?"

I love this. And I hate this. It gets right to the point of our struggle and it hurts.

If we lack Destiny Goals and have no desire to make a deeper impact in the world, we will never find our momentum flow. It will evade us and we will find that we are wasting time that could be spent changing lives.

Once we get trapped in the cycle of wasting our time on things that don't really matter it's hard to get out. We have to forcibly choose to make a big change and focus on the right things.

Everyone has a true purpose to their existence. Something that gives them joy, makes every moment count, and positively impacts the world around them. I don't have any scientific evidence for that statement, but I believe it to my core. I enjoy going to sporting events as much as the next guy, but I know that there is more to life. It's important that we fight for others and the collective well-being of the world. If we don't, we will lose, and nothing will change.

If we allow ourselves to be in a constant state of searching for happiness and fulfilment with life's pleasures, we won't be able to understand the deeper meaning and potential in our lives. We have to recognize that seeking happiness solely through entertainment is a dead end and the cause of much wasted time.

Going out on the lake to spend time with family? Great. Spending every single weekend out on the lake as a means of pleasure, with no time spent towards a bigger dream? Not so good.

Where the rubber meets the road is up you. I can't tell you how much time you should spend on each activity. What I can share is that while spending a few hours per week playing video games with my brother is something I've chosen as a top priority in my life, it can be easy for me to justify playing every single night if I am truly enjoying it.

The hard truth? Everyone is called to do more than they already are. We have so much potential to change the world, yet we often squander that potential with wasted time. We can certainly work in fun and enjoyable things in our lives to fulfill and enrich us. To truly counter wasted time and blast forward with unparalleled momentum consider searching for and acting out your true purpose in this one life.

You will find that if most of what you do every day is working towards your greater purpose, your levels of burnout will decrease, and your goal-getting momentum will become volcanic.

If you find yourself playing video games every night, try these tips first before it becomes a bad habit:

1) Pull out your journal and take notes about where you are with your Destiny Goals. Your wasted time might stem from lack of progress here. What's one SAG or BHAG you can aim towards today before you take a break?

2) Call or text someone in your family. Talk about your hopes and dreams for the world. Even better, ask them what they think you were born to do. This is a great way to get an "umm what now!?" but also makes for a great ice breaker.

3) Have an idea session: Brainstorming sessions with my wife are

one of our favorite activities to do together. We recognize we are pretty weird for this, but nothing lights up our neurons faster and gives us more energy than brainstorming about our Destiny Goals. It's a chance for us to connect on a deeper level, but also redirect our thinking and actions towards something bigger than just "what do you want for dinner tonight?"

4) Spend fifteen minutes working towards something important to you. If after fifteen minutes you need to stop and chill, no problem. Make sure to do something productive first before you jump into entertainment, even if you just got home from a long day of work. Consider this even more so if you just got home from a job you don't necessarily like.

5) Invite a friend or family member over for dinner. It's absolutely incredible how much energy we gain from being around other people, even for those of us that are introverts.

6) Pick up a new book. Reading is one of those hobbies with a very high return on investment, no matter what types of content you are reading.

7) If your brain can't handle too much thinking, restore your goal energy with an early night's sleep, a long walk, or a longer meditation session.

Fending off wasted time will propel you towards the surface of your volcano faster than you might expect. Explosive growth can occur as you learn to fend off this mightiest of foes.

Are you feeling even better now as a plan is starting to form in your mind? Using these strategies will fend off the desire to waste time before it takes hold.

Keep reading and discover more secrets to Volcanic Momentum.

Remember how I said that journaling is a great way to find momentum? I've created 25 journal prompts to get you started. You can grab them here before you move on:

www.JMRing.com/volcanic-momentum-bonuses

Strategy #4:

THE IMPORTANCE OF COMMUNITY FOR SUSTAINING MOMENTUM

"You can't create anything meaningful on an island. It takes a community of people… and lots of good coffee."

—Jenny Moates[11]

People give you energy. Even the most recluse introvert needs to be around people to avoid feeling like a zombie.

As someone that works from home, I need to constantly go out of my way in order to be around other people to gain energy after working from my office alone all week.

I love what I do, but staying in the same space all day, every day can be suffocating. I learned early on that I need to get out as much as I can and go to coffee shops. (A large portion of this book was typed on my Chromebook while sipping venti Americanos.)

I am involved in several activities that feed my need for community such as weekly lunches with my mentor, meeting with my Life Group from church, attending church, and going to boot camp workouts.

---

11 Moates, Jenny. *50 Coffees: How to Build Community (and Your Business) One Coffee at a Time.* 2017.

If not for these activities I know I would quickly lose all momentum, and getting it back would be difficult.

One of the best books I've read on the subject of building community is the book I quoted to start this chapter, *50 Coffees: How to Build Community (and Your Business) One Coffee at a Time*. This book was written by author, entrepreneur, and my good friend, Jenny Moates.

At first glance, *50 Coffees* is a book about networking, plain and simple. In actuality this book is about so much more than that. After reading the first chapter I was hooked and couldn't wait to read it from cover to cover.

It changed my perspective on building community. For a guy that usually sees results as coming only from data tracking and quantitative outcomes, building community and business growth through relationships was foreign to me.

The essence of the book is to share that building connections doesn't have to be something that scares us. We don't have to attend large networking conferences that have us awkwardly sharing our elevator pitch to the guy in the really expensive suit.

Jenny captured the essence of exactly what it means to build community through intentional effort. She set a goal of having fifty coffees with fifty different people.

Through Jenny's experiences I learned that I needed to be more intentional about my own relationship building. I needed to ask more people to go to coffee with me and build strong foundations. Not only in the hopes to grow my business, but to grow personally and learn how to give back to others.

Having other people involved in your dreams and goals will:

- Give you lasting momentum to see the goal out to the finish. If you tell a friend that you are doing something, it becomes that much harder to quit! If you keep telling people about it, you motivate yourself to completion, no matter how hard it is.

- Give you the support and accountability you need when you get stuck or lose motivation.

- Help you to see that others face similar problems and stumbling blocks as well. No one has everything figured out, and you can rest assured that someone else out there has probably gone through similar trials.

- Show you that being a support for someone else and helping them finish out their goals will be even more rewarding than hitting your own. Just by being a listening ear, we can make a profound difference in the lives of others. Wouldn't you want to be a part of that?

You can build your circle in many ways, but I'll suggest four big ones:

1) Start by asking a friend or acquaintance to coffee

2) Seek out a mentor

3) Consider joining a mastermind group

4) And last but not least, give back to others.

This list is not exhaustive for building community, but it will definitely get you started.

Your First Coffee Date

It's still a little awkward for me to ask someone, "Hey, you wanna grab coffee?" But I always look forward to the time. I don't do it as often as I should, but I know that getting to know people one-on-one is energizing and keeps me going.

Community building can be daunting or might not make sense to start right away. Maybe you are making a major life transition, still figuring out your Destiny Goals and your ultimate purpose, or have some other areas you want to focus on first. When you have made the change and pinned down your ideas, get yourself out there. Start slowly, and channel your inner tortoise if you need to, but do get out there.

To get started:

1) Ask someone out to coffee or lunch. Pick someone you work with, go to church with, or maybe even a local author or business owner. Don't make it a big thing right off the bat, just ask and see if they are interested. For example, I've asked my boot camp trainer, new pastor at my church, and most of the guys in my Life Group. Those one-on-one conversations really help to cement the existing relationship.

2) Make the only true agenda of the meeting to get to know the other person better.

3) Come prepared to talk about yourself. Most people enjoy talking about themselves, but some would rather listen.

4) Only schedule a few meet-ups at first to get your feet wet.

Find a Mentor

Having a mentor in your life that you meet with regularly is huge for growth. I am fortunate in that I've found a life mentor to guide my spiritual and relational well-being, and we have been meeting for the last year or so as of this writing.

Tom has turned into a close friend and I value the words he has spoken into my life. I would not be the person I am today without him.

But it wasn't easy to find someone that wanted to meet regularly, listen to me, AND wouldn't be afraid to speak truth in my life if need be. This kind of relationship isn't easy to find. I've found that most books fail to share how exactly to find a mentor, and with good reason! It's not like you can just make them appear and do your bidding. Because of the intimate nature of the relationship, it can be as hard as finding a spouse! (Business idea: Tinder for finding a mentor? Just sayin'. Share some of the moolah with me if that idea works out as well as I think it could.)

Your best bet for finding a mentor is to build your community and meet new people. The more you get involved and the more you interact with people in a variety of groups, the better chance you have at meeting someone that is ready to mentor you.

Once I decided to find a mentor, it took several years before it came about. It didn't happen right away. I didn't want to rush the process and I don't suggest you do either.

While you build community and search out your mentor, be patient. Read everything you can get your hands on and learn from the best. Learn from the stories of people that have been exactly where you want to go and do your best to emulate their success.

We can be mentored by someone even if we never meet them in person. This is the magic and wonder of books.

My favorite author, Mark Batterson, has changed my life in many ways, and I've never met the guy. I hope to do so one day, but until then I will devour his written words, and I will be better off for it.

Don't sit idle and wait to find the perfect person to mentor you. Seek out works from people you want to emulate, all the while keeping your eyes open for a real life opportunity.

Join a Mastermind Group

Did you know that C.S. Lewis and J.R.R. Tolkien were both part of a writing group called the Inklings?

Founded by Tolkien and Lewis, the Inklings met every Thursday night for years, reading aloud plays, manuscripts, novels, biographies, etc. The group gave critical feedback of the writer's work, all while enjoying each other's company.

Napoleon Hill defines *mastermind group* as:

"The coordination of knowledge and effort of two or more people, who work toward a definite purpose, in the spirit of harmony. No two minds ever come together without thereby creating a third, invisible intangible force, which may be likened to a third mind [the 'master' mind]."

With the time and effort put into this group by both Tolkien and Lewis, it's no wonder they created such epic works of art with their writing. They weren't writing by themselves and wondering whether or not the work they were producing was good, they were able to get immediate feedback on their works to master their craft.

Big time entrepreneurial gurus like Pat Flynn and Aaron Walker swear by mastermind groups for moving their businesses forward.

If the opportunity strikes, or you find yourself in a particular rut, a mastermind group will be an ace in the hole for your next steps.

If it sounds intriguing to you, seek out a group that is interested in reaching a certain goal. This could be a writing group like the Inklings, an online business mastermind, or a group that's focused on crushing parenthood.

Again, the more we can interact with other people, especially people interested in similar life goals, the more we will find growth and momentum.

Embrace a Generous Lifestyle

"The wise man does not lay up his own treasures. The more he gives to others, the more he has for his own."

　　—Lao Tzu

At Christmastime, I love the feeling of spending a little bit of extra time on a special gift. One year, my wife got my brother in our secret-Santa gift exchange. To really mess with him and make him work for the gifts, she dressed me up as an angel and took videos of me presenting him with clues. She then showed these videos to him on Christmas Day.

I'm not ashamed to admit that I loved it, and the voice I created for the character will live on in infamy with my family. It was ridiculous, but my brother loved the experience. We don't remember what gifts were actually given, but we remember enjoyable moments with people.

The last community-building tip I will share is to give of your time and money. Give of your time abundantly, and give your money when you can. Our blessings always return two-fold when we do this.

It can be hard to know how to help or where to serve. I know from experience that sometimes the best way to get started with giving back and helping others is to get involved anyhow and anywhere. The perfect opportunity might not present itself until you decide to take a leap.

This could be as simple as volunteering Sunday at church, or maybe you could donate to a local cause. It doesn't matter what it is, only that you give back. Opportunities to help others are often right around the corner, but you need to be looking in order to find them.

Next time you venture to bridge club, attend Wednesday night basketball, or play video games on a Friday night with old friends, keep your eyes and ears open to the need and then fill it if you can.

Nothing will fill your heart with pure joy like doing something for others, and you will be surprised at what comes back around. All of a sudden you will have a community right behind you lifting you up towards your goals.

The more lives you impact, the more you open yourself up to the possibility of that good being returned to you. This isn't karma for karma's sake; it's changing the world for the purpose of making the world a better place to live. It's about making a difference for the collective good of all people. It's about giving back and then growing as a result.

Final Thoughts on Community for Momentum

Slowly work to build a community around you and your dreams. Whether you have fifty coffees with fifty folks, start looking for a business mastermind, or maybe meet with one new person, get yourself out there and connect with people.

People make things happen. People change the world. Get involved with other people and you will blow the lids off all your goals.

Strategy #5:

WEEKLY MEETINGS FOR ABUNDANT MOMENTUM: EXECUTE THE RIGHT GOALS WEEK TO WEEK

Weekly Reviews. Wait, what?!

This is one of those pieces of advice that, when I share with people, heads almost always turn.

"Umm, you guys do what now?"

Yes friend, I am not ashamed to admit that my wife and I have weekly meetings in which we discuss our budget, schedule, and goals. We have done this for the past year, and it has been one of the best changes we've ever made. It's one of the most effective strategies for reaching goals that we've implemented, and I love it. Weekly reviews have taken our goal-getting momentum to the next level.

Despite the eye rolls and fake smiles we often get (we see you), weekly meetings are incredibly simple and explosive for growth. In fact, if I had to put my money on one takeaway from this book, this tip would be it. So listen up: Schedule weekly check-in meetings with an accountability partner. It's work, but it works. Once you find a partner and schedule weekly check-ins your momentum volcano will soar up into the heavens. Think I'm wrong? Try me.

I know it sounds about as fun as mixing tuna salad, but don't knock it until you try it. Weekly meetings take a little bit of discipline to get right, but the gains cannot be matched by any other strategy.

We currently meet every week to discuss our goals. We actually look forward to this time. The meetings are a great chance for us to reset by discussing what went well and what didn't over the last week.

It's just one way to take our dreams and desires to the next level, and it's working wonders for us so far. We suggest it to anyone reaching for just a little bit more.

Will Weekly Meetings Work for Me?

The effectiveness of weekly meetings depends on many factors, but here are some of the benefits you can expect to receive if you decide to have weekly check-ins with your partner. The meetings will:

- Clarify your vision for what you need to accomplish in the upcoming week. After your weekly meeting, you'll know exactly how to move the needle.

- Give you a chance to discuss how things went the previous week. Did you accomplish your tasks? If not, why not?

- Allow you the chance to get back on track quickly when life happens. You can choose to either not pursue the task that you're failing to accomplish, or work out why it's not going well and what you can do to fix it going forward.

- Make accountability easy. Since you are meeting with the same person every week, you will get to know the other person's goals very well and understand their true progress.

- Give you the opportunity to help each other out if you are struggling.

- Be a fun time that you look forward to. Really! Because you know your week will be filled with tasks that clearly get you closer to accomplishing your goals.

Weekly Meeting Format

Step #1: Find an Accountability Partner

To get the most out of this process, find a solid accountability partner. This is absolutely necessary because you can't have a meeting with yourself. You could ask your significant other, a good friend, or a relative you're close with to partner with you as you seek to achieve your Destiny Goals.

The "who" is flexible as long as they are committed. That being said, a spouse or partner works best, because they are often the one you spend the most time with, and your goals will often be very similar.

Step #2: Pick a Time

Decide together on a time to have the meeting. Set aside thirty minutes to an hour depending on the subject matter you decide on for your meetings. For us, Sunday afternoons work best because this time is generally free of other plans and we usually chat about the upcoming week on Sundays anyway. It's a great way to start the new week and be intentional in your plans.

Sundays are often a good time for families to reset and take a breather, so if you have a half hour to spare, then go for it.

Whatever time you choose, meet consistently at that time. You can certainly move it around if needed as things are bound to come up.

For example, sometimes Miranda and I meet Saturday night to get ahead of the game and reserve Sunday afternoon for other activities (especially during football season).

Step #3: Prepare

Prepare for your weekly meetings by getting a notebook dedicated specifically to those meetings. This will enable you to keep track of your goals and to know how you did.

It might be old school to take meeting "minutes," but it's also kind of fun and makes the meeting feel more official. Taking minutes creates a record of your goals to look back at and see how far you have come.

Before each meeting, make sure you personally brainstorm what your next week's goals will look like. You don't have to have it all laid out, but make sure you have a general idea.

Step #4: First Meeting

Spend the first meeting talking about the structure of your meetings. Ask yourselves:

- What do we want the focus of the meeting to be?
- When should we meet and how long?
- How will we delegate tasks so that they make the most sense for each person?
- How are these meetings going to help us focus on our SAGs, BHAGs, and Destiny Goals, and help us keep up the momentum to finish strong?
- How can we best help each other complete our tasks each week?
- Do we sign off on our weekly tasks with a blood offering or

is spitting into our palms and high-fiving acceptable? (Just kidding. Please don't!).

For us, the primary focus of our meetings is the budget, closely followed by weekly scheduling, and then goals. There are a lot of unknowns and flex in our budget since I work as a freelancer, so this is why we structure our check-ins to focus on finances. You can certainly focus on other subjects if that's what you need. I bring my laptop to the meeting to check our budget spreadsheet and Miranda writes down our talking points.

Having these weekly meetings has allowed both of us to know where we stand financially at all times, to make plans ahead of our money, and be in control of our spending.

After talking through the week's budget we proceed to the scheduling, and then on to individual goals. We discuss last week's goals and then make new ones for the next week.

Spend time brainstorming ideas for how you want things to go. If you need to add in rewards or punishments you can do so, but only if necessary. For us, it's enough to know that we told the other person we were going to do it, so we'd better find a way to make it happen.

We don't beat ourselves up if we don't follow through, but if we are consistently not accomplishing the goal, we know we either need to change it or resolve to get it done for real the next week.

Step #5: The Right Types of Goals (Actionable Tasks)

The goals you make for the week should be action steps you can realistically take that week to get one step closer to completing a SAG, BHAG, or Destiny Goal. The idea isn't to write down that you will definitely lose five pounds over the next week. A much better goal would be to write *how* you are going to do that.

For example, you could make it a goal (task) for the next week to go to the gym four times. This action is directly in your control. Barring unforeseen circumstances, it is likely that you can go to the gym four times this week. Losing five pounds is dependent upon a variety of circumstances and is not directly influenceable.

As outlined in *The Four Disciplines of Execution*[12] by Chris McChesney and Sean Covey, these actionable tasks are considered lead measures. A lead measure is what you put into practice to move your progress bar forward.

A lag measure, on the other hand, is the progress bar and is not directly influenceable. Lag measures are metrics, such as your weight, that you cannot directly change. You need to put lead measures into place to achieve progress on the lag measures.

Put simply: the lag measures are the goals and the lead measures are the tasks that need to be done to complete those goals.

An easy way to fail is to set weekly goals that you might not reach, or that are not dependent upon your actions.

That being said, definitely challenge yourself! Just make sure the weekly goal is contingent upon things that are in your control.

It's a subtle difference but an important one. I can do things to sell books, but I can't sell books directly, so weekly goals should be actionable items in nature.

---

12 *The 4 Disciplines of Execution.* FranklinCovey, www.franklincovey.com/Solutions/Execution/4-disciplines.html.

Step #6: Be Consistent

Meet every week, no matter what. Make time for this weekly check-in and don't quit.

If things get busy and you aren't able to meet? Time out! I call BS. Make time for it. Make time for yourself and your partner to flourish. It's a facade that we are too busy. We are only shifting our priorities. Never believe that you are too busy for something that will help you to move forward in your goals.

Go at your own pace, but make sure you meet every week, even if it means meeting for only fifteen minutes.

If this still sounds utterly depressing, here are some ways you can make this a fun activity:

1) Attach the new habit to a habit you already do well, like date night or working out together. Do the meeting before or after these activities to create the habit.

2) If you end up going on a long car ride with your partner you can discuss things in the car instead of listing to music. Miranda and I have done this several times and it works out well.

3) If it helps, make a special meal or snack to celebrate. We call our weekly meetings Sheetz, Sheets, and Sheets. Why? Because the initial plan was to grab Sheetz food (made-to-order gas station food), wash our sheets, and take notes on sheets of paper. We don't do any of these things anymore, but it truly helped to make it a habit.

4) Go for a walk or maybe even start up the meeting with a dance party. Whatever it is, attach something fun and unique to your meetings in order to make the habit stick.

For more ideas and advice about weekly meetings, you can listen to our podcast episode here in which Miranda and I discuss these meetings in greater depth: www.JMRing.com/freedom-cast-episode-five-weekly-meetings-stellar-growth.

There you have it. This is the next step to reaching your dreams and unlocking your ultimate potential.

Strategy #6:

FAIL FORWARD: GAIN MASSIVE MOMENTUM BY DITCHING THE PLAN AND DIVING IN

"I have not failed. I've just found 10,000 ways that won't work."
—Thomas Edison

When I was graduating from the 8th grade I volunteered to play a short rendition of "Amazing Grace" on my trumpet during graduation. I was sweating from my ears as I walked up to the stage to play the two-minute rendition that I had been practicing for months. It was a version I learned myself by ear and never had to write down. I owned that song every time I practiced it!

Except this time.

The sounds that came from my trumpet would have made a banshee cringe. I couldn't form a single note and left the stage crying. I bawled in front of an auditorium packed to the brim for my 8th grade graduation. What a fool I made of myself.

But thankfully I had some good friends, an amazing music teacher, and a supportive community at the school. After calming down I gave it another try and crushed it.

The crowd went wild and gave me a standing ovation. I think my parents even led an attempt at the wave. I didn't even care that they were probably just cheering that I didn't leave to go cry again!

My absolute worst fear came true, and things still turned out okay.

Learning from mistakes is the surest way to build momentum and crush a goal, as long as we use the experience as a *learning moment* instead of feeling bad for ourselves.

I could have quit that night and vowed never to play the trumpet again, but I was given a second chance and redeemed myself. I moved forward through the failure and used it as a learning opportunity.

The truth is we will either strive forward or putz backwards. Remember the neutral myth? There is no middle ground. There is no status quo, only positive or negative momentum.

For most of my life I've had very little forward momentum, and while I've avoided an accumulation of too many embarrassing stories like the one above, I think I've most often failed by *not* failing; I haven't been able to use failure as a springboard to growth until recently.

I used to be clouded by so many questions:

- How should I spend the majority of my time?
- Should I go to college?
- How do I make a girl like me?
- What do I want to do with my life?

I realized that I wasn't taking action, and that I was failing a lot but not using it to move forward. I was failing for nothing and not growing. This is failing backward, not forward.

What a mess I made of a lot of things. What a mess I had to dig myself out of.

In high school I did well, but didn't apply myself fully. I made a few close friends and then spent the rest of my free time in self-serving endeavors like video games or tennis.

Fast-forward to senior year of college. My girlfriend of six months broke up with me and broke my heart. I had already accrued tons of college-loan debt for a degree I didn't have any desire to use, and I once again spent most of my time playing video games, and got fat in the process.

After college wasn't any better. I had to borrow money from my roommate to pay the first rent bill in our new apartment. I hate thinking about that, and I don't even like sharing it, but it's where I was at the time. I was poor, without a plan, and overweight.

My then-girlfriend, now wife, still loved me somehow, and for that I am forever in her debt. But I didn't have a lot of respect for myself. I was floundering with no real plan for building a future. Without the structure of college I was losing momentum quickly. I was falling backward and going nowhere. I wasn't using the failure for growth.

Can you relate?

Luckily God had a plan for me. He has a plan for you too, but you need to take a step towards that plan, and keep stepping and failing every day.

A Grander Plan

"Success seems to be connected with action. Successful people keep moving. They make mistakes, but they don't quit."
—Conrad Hilton

The day I realized that I was missing out on my grander plan is firmly planted within my mind. I was at the Global Leadership Summit (The GLS) the summer I turned 25. The GLS is a leadership conference that aims to encourage and empower leaders of all kinds to lead their businesses, churches, and organizations with the utmost care and attention.

I can't give you a quote from that day that changed me; rather, I only know that after I left my mindset was changed. Legacy mattered. My life mattered. What we do in this life really matters.

Why had it taken so long to sink in? I wish I knew, but at 25 I was ready to go. I was ready to make a big difference in the world. I was ready to stop spending so much time worrying about my own wants and needs and ask how I could be part of a grander plan.

I didn't know for sure what that grander plan was, but I felt more aligned with God's heart and plan for me than I ever had. I felt as if I was getting closer to finding the purpose for my life.

Ready. Set. Fail?

"You don't learn to walk by following rules. You learn by doing and falling over."

—Richard Branson

I was finally ready to dive in and fail forward. I'd be the person that failed a lot, but instead of remaining stuck, I'd use failure to propel me forward.

No longer would I be an "I'll do it someday" kind of guy. I was ready to become a man of action and forge a life that mattered.

And holy cow, was it hard. My momentum in most aspects of my life was stuck in mud and sliding downhill. Just stopping the sludge was hard enough, but now I had to surge ahead!? It felt impossible. I didn't know if I would make it.

Learning to get finances in order, lose weight, and set goals was grueling and I failed often. But therein lies the secret. Failing bred success, if for no other reason than knowing one thing not to do.

Failing forward is not easy by any means, but it does get easier with time. Ease yourself into it with one fail at a time and grow from there.

In his book *Bluefishing: The Art of Making Things Happen*[13], author and entrepreneur Steve Sims shares that the best way to learn is to dive in and get going. He found at a young age that he would easily fly by his peers because he was willing to get dirty and fail multiple times while others were still planning. He learned more by trying and failing than by planning alone.

He shares often throughout the book a quote his father shared with him one day while walking along:

"Son, no one ever drowned by falling in the water. They drown by staying there."

Steve believes, and so do I, that taking risks and trying new things is the path to higher learning. We certainly should have a plan, but if our tendency is to overplan without trying, we need to err on the side of failure and just go for it.

He went from being a literal bricklayer, to making people's wildest dreams come true. He has gotten people down to the Titanic, orchestrated a marriage by the Pope in the Vatican, and connected individuals with powerful business moguls like Elon Musk.

---

13   Sims, Steve. *Bluefishing: The Art of Making Things Happen*. Gallery Books, 2018.

He is now changing lives for folks because he learned to think outside the box and look beyond what was thought possible. Some of the stuff he has done for people seems impossible, yet he did it. His strategy of making win-win situations and daring to do the impossible has earned him respect and admiration from his clients.

He has learned the art of getting to know what people really want, and then figuring out how to make it happen. I recommend reading his book, as it helped grow my outside-the-box thinking, showed me the value of digging deeper with people, and reaffirmed my belief that "no" usually only means "not right now."

"I have always believed if you get a 'NO' in a conversation, you're either asking the wrong person or you're asking the wrong question."
—Steve Sims

Take a risk, fail, and don't let rejection bring you down. Don't take no for an answer.

Paralysis by Analysis

Ever heard of paralysis by analysis? It's a killer whale in the goal-achieving ocean. It strikes and drags you down under before you even have a chance to take a deep breath.

Don't fall victim to this dangerous monster.

Spend time making goals and planning, but not so much time that all you do is plan! Take action and either find success or failure. If you succeed? Great! Keep on going. If you fail? Pick yourself up, dust yourself off, and get back in the game.

Too often in my own life, and from stories I've heard of other people's struggles, we let the fear of what could be dictate our actions.

Shouldn't the fear of inaction be just as strong, or stronger? Shouldn't we be more afraid of what might happen if we do nothing?

Just as a baby learns to walk by falling over countless times, so too must we forsake deliberations and go for it. You'll fall on your butt more often than not, but when you do start walking, the world opens up before you.

Stop planning to go on a diet "when the holidays are over" and make a healthy choice right now. Your sugar dragon always has a "special reason to celebrate."

Take an action step for your new business venture and put an offer on a storefront. Throw caution to the wind and talk to that hottie that just made herself at home at the workstation across from you.

You might fail to lose any weight, your business might go under, and that hottie will probably turn you down. Failing is no reason to fear such things. Failure counterintuitively creates confidence and experience where planning cannot.

Stop fearing the myriad ways things can go wrong and instead consider what would happen if things go right.

I want you to chew on these words John Maxwell shares in his book *No Limits: Blow the CAP Off Your Capacity*:

"You will fail. And that's not just OK, it's essential. Without resilience, the first failure is also the last—because it's final. Those who are excellent at their work have learned to comfortably coexist with failure. The excellent fail more often than the mediocre. They begin more. They attempt more. They attack more. Mastery lives quietly atop a mountain of mistakes."

That sure makes me feel better about my own failures. Thanks, John!

You could plan a thousand ways to achieve a desired outcome but you have no idea if it's going to work. The truth is that more often than not, first attempts fail, and fail hard. Second and third attempts will soon surpass even the most well thought-out and detailed plan because you are actively learning.

Take book launching for example. I am ten times better at it than I used to be, and now I help other authors get it right on the first time and forgo a lot of the mistakes I used to make. Even still, new authors make errors, and it's only through those errors that they learn what to do and what not to do.

When I launched my first book, my attention was all over the place. I was like a little kid in a candy store with a Benjamin in my hand. I wanted the best candy, but ended up just getting the Twizzlers. I don't even like Twizzlers!

Too often we want to *talk* about making a change when *doing* something about it would be a far better venture. Whiteboards are worthless if you don't actually do the things you write on them.

Ask yourself what you could fail towards today and then get started. Don't spend weeks making a plan; put your best foot forward and go for it.

You might just be surprised by what you find on the other end.

Becoming a Person of Action

"When you take risks, you learn that there will be times when you succeed and there will be times when you fail, and both are equally important."

—Ellen DeGeneres

Today, I'm obsessed with goals. The old Jordan was content playing videos games every night for hours. Present-day Jordan is way more on track. I'm living every day trying to work towards my purpose. I still fail all the time (just ask my boot camp trainer Chad when I still can't balance while doing lunges), but I am able to get back up that much faster.

I wish I had started sooner, but all I can do is move forward from this current moment, make mistakes, increase my momentum in the best direction I know, and keep on pushing.

Even still, my modus operandi is to stop and question every decision. I constantly have to fight these battles. Even the decision of whether or not to do the dishes right away can be a struggle of epic proportions.

Conquer the part of you that says, "wait a second, I don't feel like doing that," and run towards action. Deliberate when necessary ("Hmm, this 100-foot dive into rocky waters might kill me"), but only say no if there is an immediate danger or you know of a better option.

Learn to take risks and dive headfirst into action. You won't regret the massive progress you will see in your life and in the lives of those around you.

Fail early. Fail hard. Find massive success and contentment in your life by doing.

Good luck failing, partner.

Strategy #7:

CREATE SERENDIPITY TO KEEP UP MOMENTUM

One aspect of serendipity to bear in mind is that you have to be looking for something in order to find something else.

—Lawrence Block

How do you open doors and find new opportunities? Just ask.

Asking sounds too simple, yet it works more often than you would expect. Doors will slam in your face, but now we know that's a win too.

I used to be afraid to ask anything of anyone because I didn't want to hear "no." Man, was I missing out!

My thinking changed when I read a book called *View From the Top: Living a Life of Significance*[14] by Aaron Walker. Aaron is a serial entrepreneur that at 28 retired from his day job with more money than he would ever need. His life mantra has since become part of my own: *"Fear missing an opportunity more than you fear failure."*

Aaron never let the answer "no" stop him from continuing to press

---

14   Walker, Aaron. *View from the Top: Living a Life of Significance.* Morgan James, 2017.

forward. If someone told him "no," he took it as "not right now." Maybe it seems like a subtle difference, but I don't think so.

Asking is not about bothering or badgering those that say no; it's about our perspective on the matter. Our perspective tells us whether we:

1) Fail miserably, or:

2) The timing isn't right at the current moment.

Having an attitude that believes "not right now" is the way Aaron took on life's challenges. It's the way I want to live. It's what we all should strive for.

There is no reason to live with a fear of failure. The fear of failure often prevents us from getting anything done.

Don't let the fear of hearing no stop you from planting seeds and putting yourself out there.

Creating Serendipity

In 2016, I reached out to the self-publishing services company Archangel Ink that I had used for cover design and formatting for my books.

I told them in a short email that I enjoyed working with them and that if something came up, I would love for them to consider bringing me on their team.

They had nothing right away, and I wasn't expecting it. I had NO experience in self-publishing other than what I had done for my own books, but I could tell they were a company I'd enjoy working for based on my communication with them.

Lo and behold, in early 2017 they reached out and took me on to do audio editing. That went well, so later on they hired me to be their book launch and marketing coach for authors.

The timing was perfect, as I had just moved on from another job, and I was looking for something I could do from home.

That little ask from a year earlier created a serendipitous moment. I don't believe this was sheer luck. It's a direct result of an action I took before the need arose. Asking didn't give me an immediate yes, but it created a serendipitous moment later on that changed my life.

Don't be afraid to plant seeds. They might never grow. They might turn into massive trees that grow money. Don't you want to take that chance?

Want another example? A situation that was a flat-out no turned into an "Oh wait, yes!"

For the launch of my book *Book Launch Gladiator*, I reached out to a website called Instafreebie and asked them if they would feature my book in their newsletter. At first they said no. Just a flat-out, "No we won't do that for your book."

Well, that sucked. Until I dug a little further, asked why, and showed them my stats.

My second email paid off, and they told me they hadn't really read the first email, and that they would love to feature my book.

My book was featured in one of their daily emails, and it resulted in an extra two hundred email sign ups. Two hundred emails for a simple ask is a bargain! This simple act of persistence worked out in my favor.

Why didn't they read my incredible first outreach email? Well, besides the fact that maybe it wasn't as incredible as I thought it was, it doesn't matter. Asking why and digging a little deeper was the turning point in this situation.

Does the ask always work out this way? Of course not. I continue to submit for feature deals on BookBub (the holy grail of book promotion services for authors) and never get featured. Most authors don't. But it doesn't mean I won't keep trying. One day, if I am lucky, they will feature one of my books, and I will shout a victorious "YES!!" for all of Starbucks to hear.

There's no harm in asking, other than hurt pride and a few wasted minutes. We will be better off if we can learn to handle rejection.

One of my favorite quotes of all time is something my wife once said:

"I think I need more rejection in my life."

The comment stunned me. I stared back at her dumbfounded. Miranda was stating that she needed to hear the word "no" more often in order to build up resilience.

No only means "not right now." If you can keep this perspective, the word "no" won't have the same painful meaning for you. If you can take a "no" answer in stride you will be better off for it.

Note: You don't need to then tell the person "Oh I'll just have to keep pestering you, I know that no only means no right now!" This will come off as salesy or rude. Tell them okay and move on. You can ask leading questions if the response isn't negative, but if the "no" reaction is strong, just wait for another day. It's beyond the scope of this book to share exactly what to say to others when they say no, but remember to focus on the well-being of the relationship and you should be fine.

If you find yourself afraid to ask, ask yourself what might be holding you back. Is it your fear that someone will tell you no? Or is it an irrational fear of what might happen to you if they say no?

Often, our irrational fears can stop us from taking bold action. What's the worst that can happen? The person is rude, yells at us, or never speaks to us again.

Asking "what's the best that can happen?" is a much more useful question. Remember what Wayne Gretzky said: "*We miss 100% of the shots we don't take.*"

Let me share one final example here as I think this is such a powerful point. I'm still learning the art of just asking, but it has been such a useful tool in my life kit that I want to share it with you.

Again, for *Book Launch Gladiator*, I reached out to famous indie author Steve Scott for an endorsement. You know what he said? Yes. I was freaking out when I got the email back. He wrote me a great review, too.

I could have just written it off and never asked him. I could have thought it wouldn't even be worth asking someone that receives tons of requests just like mine.

I could have answered for him and not bothered to ask. Instead I did ask, and the results were great.

What do you have to lose? As an author, entrepreneur, businessman, or whatever your job title, you will need to jump at some point.

I get it. I struggle with even calling someone on the phone. I hate thinking I might bother them. But I know that I can't let this fear stop me forever. Sometimes you have to call and see what happens.

The key lesson is learning to go with the flow and to take chances along the way.

You can start small by asking for a discount on your coffee. Scared that the barista might laugh at you and tell you no? Does it even matter? Just ask and see what happens.

The absolute worst that might happen is that they might spit in your coffee, but I doubt it.

The best that can happen? The employee says "sure!" and gives you the coffee for free. Better yet, every time you come in from now on you get free coffees because you know you can. Absurd? Maybe… but it's still a possibility.

How's that for momentum building? You ask a question and no longer have to pay for coffee. Huge win!

Once you unleash the power of the ask anything can happen. Your rent could be slashed in half, you could get free cinnamon twists at Taco Bell (I did this once, and got free twists for my birthday), or you could land a dream job. Do the thing that separates the wheat from the chaff and put yourself out there.

Take note that during the ask you never want to delve into being too demanding for anything. If they can't give you a discount, make a joke and move on. Pay for your coffee and try next time.

Lest anyone thinks at this point that you should ask, ask, ask to get, get, get, think about this: It's important to remember that this is an exercise for you to get better at sharing your desires and boosting your own personal momentum.

Always be courteous and look for opportunities to give back. Focus on the relationship at all times. If someone is getting worked up at your ask, back off and either try again later or drop it. Learn to read social signals.

You might get caught up in the fun that comes with these new experiences, but never forget that you are dealing with real people who have feelings, wants, and needs. Your gain should never come with someone else's loss.

Once you get better at asking for these types of things, ask for bigger favors. Get used to putting yourself out there.

Ask for reviews for your new book, ask your boss for a raise, or ask your bank to forgive your student loans. (I recognize this one in insane. I tried it once and it didn't work. But it didn't get me down since they only told me "not right now," remember?).

The worst thing that can happen is that they say no, no, and no. But certain things will not be a no forever.

When you ask your boss, he might say you will get one in six months. If you had waited six months, he probably would have said the same thing, thus totaling a whole year for your raise.

Think about that for a second. You just cut your time between raises in half, all because you asked NOW as opposed to when the timing was perfect.

The ask is just one more secret to gaining momentum in life. Asking keeps you ahead of the game. Don't wait for things to happen to you. Make things happen. Your boss is not going to give you a raise just for fun. No, he will wait until you ask and then start the countdown.

Remember the old saying "Nice guys finish last?" Taken at its core it means that passive people won't win, and I agree with it 100%.

You can learn to ask and still be a good person. Learn to reduce passivity to surge ahead.

Asking gets the ball rolling and the momentum in place for you to succeed.

I wouldn't be where I am today If I didn't have the courage to plant these seeds and just ask.

I will leave you with this incredible quote from *Orison Swett Marden*:

"Don't wait for extraordinary opportunities. Seize common occasions and make them great. Weak men wait for opportunities; strong men make them."

Good luck to you in your continued goal to increase momentum.

Strategy #8:

HOW TO CREATE TIME: GET MORE DONE BY SAYING NO AND MASTERING YOUR PRIORITIES

"The key is not to prioritize what's on your schedule, but to schedule your priorities."

—Stephen Covey

Let's talk about how to create time.

Time is the great equalizer. No one has more time than anybody else in any given day. 24 hours in one day, 168 hours a week, 720 hours per month. It's our responsibility to choose what we do with that time, and to utilize that time in the greatest way.

With 720 hours per month:

- 33% (240 hours) is spent sleeping (assuming a generous eight hours per night).

- Another 22% is for working.

- Commuting for work (3%).

- Prepping food and eating (Just under 3%), and;

- A whopping two hours a day on social media (8.3%) (Unless

you're a teen, then the average goes up to nine hours per day: 37.5%).

After sleeping, working, commuting, eating, and social media you only have 221 hours (30.7%) left in your month. This is just about 7.3 hours per day you have to play with, with less time on work days and more time on days off (generally).

You can go way more in depth with this study, and others have done so, including this American time use study (see footnote)[15]

This last 30.7% of time is for everything else: exercise, housework, yard work, side hustles, taking care of the kids, working towards Destiny Goals, reading, watching TV, and more. You must fit every other part of your life around your daily obligations, duties, and commitments.

Time doesn't relent or give us a break. Every minute wasted is a page burnt out of a book. You can't turn back (unless your name is Doc Brown) and you can't stop it. The one and only thing we can do is to *"decide what to do with the time that is given to us"* (Gandalf from *The Lord of the Rings.*)

If we can learn to prioritize our time by saying yes to the right things, and no to the wrong things, we will maximize the time we have here on this Earth. We will create time by shifting priorities.

This is the secret to time creation, and we will hash out how to make it a reality. This isn't a blueprint for a time machine; instead, this chapter is a guide to organizing your life around what matters.

---

15 "American Time Use Survey Summary." U.S. Bureau of Labor Statistics, U.S. Bureau of Labor Statistics, 28 June 2018, www.bls.gov/news.release/atus.nr0.htm.

Shifting the Busyness Mindset

To create time, we must stop saying to ourselves, "I can't do that, I'm too busy." Own that you can't do it because it's not a priority in your life at the moment. Busyness is a facade for fear, avoidance, and misplaced priorities.

Shifting our mindset begins as soon as you wake up every day. Ask yourself: Are you going to be "busy" today or are you going to make time for what matters most?

It might involve saying no to sleeping in so you can work on your side hustle. It might mean skipping a day of work to reconnect with your spouse. It very well could include selling the Xbox so you are freed up to enjoy the outdoors more regularly.

It means looking at life with a different lens than you are used to. Analyze your daily schedule with an open mind and reduce the activities that don't contribute to your overall goals. Make sure your tasks line up with what you want your life to become.

A word of caution: if you say yes to an activity, keep your word. Strive to finish out a task you committed to doing.

My dad once sent me a copy of his new book to edit. I kept telling myself I was too busy to get to it. The manuscript sat on my counter for thirteen weeks and I had yet to start it. I took over three months to read it and send back my edits. Ouch. The memory hurts to think about. I should not have taken that long.

While I did have a lot on my plate, I could have shifted priorities and finished it up faster for him. I could have made it a habit to read for ten minutes a day until I finished the task.

In hindsight, I didn't make editing the book a priority. Once I realized this and shifted my thinking, I got it done right away and sent it off to him. I realized that "I'm too busy" was just an excuse I was telling myself.

I needed to shift that priority to a higher level, cut out the other distractions, and get the work done. My stalling meant I spent less time in front of the TV and less time writing my own projects in order to get the job done.

This is the memory that serves as a reminder for me. I'm sure if you think about it, you might have one of your own.

Yes? Or No? When to Say Which

I am sure that while reading this you are thinking, "Okay, but how do you do this in practice? How do you let your priorities govern your actions?"

The answer? Cold hard determination, grit, and lots of mistakes. Of course, knowing what your priorities are helps too.

Many times our priorities are not clear, especially for competing top-level priorities. How do you decide whether to go to your son's chess tournament or your daughter's math meet that happen to both fall on a Tuesday night at seven p.m.... thirty miles apart?

You make the best of it and do what you can. It's impossible to do everything and to be everywhere when competing top-level priorities butt heads.

The above example is a rare occurrence. Far more common are situations where the right answer might not be immediately clear, but when you think in terms of priorities, there is a clear winner. Some examples:

- I have two missed calls; who should I call back first, my brother or my wife?

- Do I take a break tonight or finish out the work project that's due soon?

- Would it be a better choice to have a healthy dinner (fitness priority) or eat a whole pizza over the sink like a rat? (Fun priority)

- Chocolate or vanilla? (just kidding, we all know vanilla is the clear winner ;))

- Should I check and respond to work email or watch the kids while my wife makes dinner?

- Should I go to church today or catch up on all the housework I've been neglecting?

When have important items in your life slunk to the bottom, and trivial tasks somehow wormed their way to the top?

Finding the balance in our daily life isn't easy, but when we are clear about our priorities, these types of decisions become easier. If we know our priorities without even thinking about them, then we can make the right choice despite tough situations.

We all have a lot on our plates, and there are things we either have to postpone or say no to. Master the art of saying no to the wrong things to say yes to the right things.

Remember the importance of finishing a task you agree to, but also realize that most people will be very gracious if you ask for more time, or for a rain check.

Don't convince yourself that you're too busy for the important things in your life. Examine your priorities and take a top-down approach.

For example, here are my priorities:

1) Relationships:

    a) God

    b) Wife

    c) Family

    d) Friends

2) Work:

    a) Top-paying work

    b) Most enjoyable work

    c) Side projects

3) Fun:

    a) Reading

    b TV

    c) Video Games

    d) Hiking

    e) Etc.

Having a good idea of what your priorities are is how you best manage time. You might have these in your head, but I suggest writing them down too, as writing them down in a concrete list makes them more real.

Just recently my wife and I weren't connecting as easily as we normally do. There seemed to be no quantifiable issue, but we felt off.

After talking, we realized that other commitments in our lives were taking a higher priority. Once this fact hit us, we took a day for us and said no to previous commitments.

We make our marriage a top priority, but life got in the way and forced us to take a step back and re-examine to make sure we either give it time right now, or make a plan to do so in the future.

As hard as it is, examining and giving ample time to your top priorities is not only advisable, it's also necessary to prevent your entire tree of priorities from crashing down around you. This doesn't mean ignoring everything that's not a top priority (those dishes won't wash themselves!), but if it comes between daily housework or the need to reconnect relationally, the dishes can wait.

Lower-tier tasks are important and can often provide a good foundation for the higher-level priorities, but there are times when vacuuming needs to be put off to tomorrow so you can have time for what matters now.

Make sure the top shelf is good to go before you prioritize anything on the lower tier. It's not an easy thing to do, but learn to recognize these trends in your own life to adjust course as needed. Strike a balance here by constantly reevaluating how much time you are spending on the tasks and activities that matter most.

As a quick and helpful exercise, list out the three activities beyond work, sleep, and eating that you spend the most time doing.

You might be surprised to find out if you answer honestly: TV, video games, and Facebook scrolling might be the biggest time culprits!

As a caveat, there are many times when level of importance shifts and you have to go to an important meeting vs. watching your daughter's soccer game. Just don't let these standalone circumstances become the norm.

Master Your Priorities

By now you are in agreement that priorities are of utmost importance. Without them, you can't get the right things done, you will become busy doing all the wrong things, and overwhelm will come for you.

Mastering your priorities starts with asking yourself some tough questions and then being up front and honest with the answers.

One simple way to start is by filling out a priority tree which you can download here as part of the companion guide: www.JMRing.com/volcanic-momentum-bonuses.

It might appear simple at first, but basing every yes or no decision on the priority tree can help create time for what's important.

The top priority is what you hold most dear. These are the tasks, responsibilities, or relationships that are the most important and demand your highest attention. For example:

- God
- Spouse
- Family
- Running a non-profit
- Business ownership
- Planting a church
- Building a foundation to help cure cancer

Mid-level priorities are important, but if a need from one of the above comes knocking, you will have to say no to these and say yes to the top level. They might look something like:

- Job and income

- Community involvement
- Relationships with friends
- Writing a book
- Eating healthy
- Getting enough exercise

Bottom-level priorities are still very important (as they are still priorities) but only cast your attention on them as long as none of your higher-level priorities are pleading for attention.

These include:

- Recreational activities
- Get-togethers with friends
- Side hustles
- Cleaning the house
- Reading

Some of these examples might shift up and down for you depending on life circumstance. Maybe your recent checkup didn't go so well? Bump up healthy eating and fitness into the top-level priority so you can be around to add "play with your grandkids" to your list later on in life.

This exercise reveals where you want to spend your time, and how you can create time and margin in your life.

You have the power to choose what you do with your life and mastering priorities is a great first step. It allows you to create a margin to be able to have time for the people and activities you care about most.

Finding Balance

In all of this, you must find a balance. Take on too much and you will fail. Take on too little and you might end up disappointed with your accomplishments in this one life.

With life comes trials. You will find success mixed with great failure in the journey. Balance is discovered by living life with this motto in mind:

"Pray as though everything depended on God. Work as though everything depended on you"

— Saint Augustine

Trust that God will see you through, but don't use this as an excuse to not do something with your life. Be bold with your time and create enough of it to do the things you know you need to do, but still find that balance between work and play. It won't be easy, but work at it and you might just find new contentment and enjoyment in this amazing, albeit very challenging, world.

Time-Creation Takeaways

I'd like to suggest the following five takeaways from this chapter:

1) Value what little time you have available to you by making the most of every minute you have.

2) Recognize that busyness is a facade. No one is too busy for something; you choose where to put your time.

3) Take a good hard look at your own priorities and determine what matters most to you.

4) Say no to lower-level activities if necessary to free up precious time to focus on the higher-level items.

5) Strike a balance by working hard while depending on God to see you through.

Strategy #9:

DON'T LET OTHERS GET YOU DOWN: TAKE FEEDBACK LIKE A CHAMP BY MASTERING YOUR PERSONAL FILTER

"Go, son! It's gone! You just hit a home-run, keep running!" my coach yelled.

It was the last game of a long season of Little League. I wasn't the best player on my team, and the bench and I quickly became best friends, but I had fun getting at least a few at-bats every game.

The last game of the season came quickly and it was my turn to head up to the plate. I took a hack at the first pitch and PING! The ball flew over the fence faster than a hedgehog collecting gold coins.

Had I really just hit a home run? Did my haphazard swing and terrible stance just barely manage to hit that little ball out of the park?

Yup. It was amazing. I'll never forget the moment as I stood there dumbfounded at what I had just done. When my senses returned and I heard my coach yelling, I ran the bases as fast as I could, touched home plate, and was immediately surrounded by my stunned but celebratory teammates. I still have the signed ball almost twenty years later.

There is nothing that compares to the feeling of running around the bases after hitting a home-run. As hitting is probably the most difficult thing to do in all sports, I was ecstatic.

How did a little kid go from struggling to hold a bat, to hitting a home-run at the end of the year?

The answer is simple: I accepted and acted on feedback throughout the year. I used every criticism I received to improve my stance and my swing.

I have always been adept at taking criticism and feedback and learning to grow from it. I am blessed with this and wouldn't give it up for anything.

As the universe has an annoying way of compensating, I can't dribble a basketball worth a lick, and I am so bad with directions I can visit a place ten times and STILL not know how to get there. I will even shamefully admit that I never graduated from the medium difficulty on *Guitar Hero*.

But luckily, ever since an early age, I have been "coachable." Once, I even won the coaches award trophy in Little League. When I started the season I couldn't hit the ball, field, or throw very far, but man I could take direction all right! And my season ended on a high note with the home-run.

I have never been all that talented, or for that matter that great at anything besides *Halo 2* and making apple pie, but I sure can take direction and feedback and use it to grow.

Every time I struck out, every time I let a ball go through my legs, I would seek help and feedback on how I could improve.

I still let the ball go through my legs whenever I am on the softball field, but gimme a break… I'm better than I used to be!

The Hidden Talent

Feedback is the hidden talent for those of us that find ourselves lacking ability. We can utilize feedback to grow and move beyond our limited natural capabilities. We can use critiques to figure out why we can't hit the ball, why our writing is poor, or even why our marriage might be struggling.

Learning to admit that we don't know exactly what to do is one of the major rules of the momentum game. Instead of staying down and feeling bad about yourself and your progress, you can use feedback to move forward from a place of strength and empowerment.

But no amount of feedback does any good for us if we are unable to move past the initial emotional struggle of self-doubt and shame.

The truth is that constructive feedback, no matter how gently given, usually hurts. It never feels good to have someone tell you that, in essence, what you did was just plain wrong.

Check out this feedback from my boss about three years ago:

"You aren't doing as well as you think you are."

To continue on the baseball metaphors, that came out of left field.

I was crushed. I was given very little context, and we never followed up after the fact.

It was wrong of him to give flippant feedback and not follow through with an explanation. But we can't control others; we can only control our reaction.

His delivery was not meant to hurt my feelings, but neither did he bother to recognize that he might be wrong. Instead it felt like an attack on me personally. It was beyond unhelpful, but such is a lot of feedback we have to face.

I had to deal with it. I had to take it for what it was and try to find a way to apply it, like it or not.

We aren't responsible for how others choose to give us feedback. The only thing that we can directly control is what we do with that feedback.

After a Good Cry...

I am not afraid to admit that I cried like a little baby that day. A 24-year-old guy who thought he was doing well with the company was callously told that he wasn't all that.

Can I say "ouch" again?

Ouch!

I was hurt and I couldn't help but feel the pain of the feedback. But I also knew I had to analyze it and do with it what I could. My coachable nature wouldn't allow me to do anything less.

The key to All This? Cultivating a Personal Filter.

Here's what to do the next time you need to process tough feedback:

1) **Shut down** your thoughts and let the feedback breathe. Don't act on the critique or respond to the critic right away. It might cause you to cry or otherwise feel emotional, and that's okay. Let it affect you, then rest and come back to it when it's not affecting you as much.

2) **Repair** your filter and process the feedback with mindful meditation or journaling. What truths does the feedback have? Where is the feedback way off base? What is your honest interpretation?

3) **Upgrade** your personal filter by talking with close family and friends. Ask them their honest opinions of the feedback you received. Not all will tell you the truth, especially if they can tell you were really hurt by it, but if you are honest with yourself you should be able to glean truth from their reactions.

After the tough feedback I received, it turned out that my personal filter was in need of a solid shutdown (the cry), a repair (more crying and thinking), and an upgrade (discussion with family and friends).

The first step was letting the feedback in, all the way to my heart. I think this step is where a lot of people put up walls to avoid pain. I don't blame those that do this, but if we refuse all feedback we limit growth and stymie momentum. If you put up impenetrable walls that don't allow for any feedback, you are only doing yourself a disservice in the long run. Feedback is the precursor to growth.

On the other hand, if you don't have your own personal filter in place to use the feedback appropriately, you end up hurting yourself for no reason.

After receiving the feedback from my boss I took it to heart, but then began to see it for what it was. I had to process it and take a rested look at it. Because I decided to chew on the criticism, and then ask others for their feedback on the criticism, I was able to ascertain the truth, and put the matter behind me.

In this case, he was wrong. I knew exactly how good I was doing, and my co-workers and subordinates all echoed my thoughts when I asked them about my performance.

If meant in a good way, feedback in general is usually spot on, and we should readily accept it and utilize it to bring about change within ourselves. But we do need to be careful of those that don't necessarily have our best interests at heart, or don't have the ability to see the situation clearly.

If your spouse tells you that you need to pay more attention to her instead of looking at your phone during dinner, you'd better take that feedback seriously and put the phone away.

If your boss tells you that you need to get better at answering emails promptly, and you KNOW that you always answer right away, tuck that feedback away into the circular file (the trash can) and forget about it.

Learn to master your personal filter so you can take in the feedback that rings true, and forget the rest.

It never gets easy, but it does get easier with time and repetition.

A Step Further

Not only should we be ready to accept feedback when it is given to us, but we should seek it out.

I know what you are thinking: That's crazy!

Most people don't do it. But in my experience, a good rule of thumb is that if most people don't do it, it might just be a good thing. (Except for the obvious, like cliff jumping or swimming with sharks because that's about as crazy as calling someone on the phone).

It may be hard to do, but I've found that seeking out quality feedback has worked wonders for me in my personal and professional lives. When you can have an open discussion with your boss about their expectations for you, it makes the yearly review quite a bit easier overall since your expectations have been discussed all year long.

Ask your boss how you could improve, ask your spouse what you could be doing better, or ask a friend what they think you could generally improve on. Make it specific if you want to dig deep, or ask a general question to get your feet wet.

Just like getting a vaccination, the more you expose yourself and your own personal filter to feedback, the more you will grow. Seek out feedback, build upon your personal filter, and never look back.

Momentum will find you and you will start to explode ever more forcefully towards your goals.

Before you move on, go here to download the companion guide for this book. I share the nine strategies for momentum together on a one-pager, with links to motivational videos for added encouragement: www.JMRing.com/volcanic-momentum-bonuses.

Section Three:

NEVER LOSE STEAM

GOAL ACCOMPLISHED. NOW WHAT?

"Yes! I lost the last ten pounds!"

"Woo-hoo! I landed my dream job!"

"Hallelujah! I finished vacuuming my car!" (Seriously though, this one deserves the space here, right?)

What do you do after accomplishing your goal? Is this the end?

If you hope to maintain forward momentum and continue to grow, this can't be the end. Growth is not about reaching one endpoint; it's about recognizing that as long as we draw breath we have value to give. To grow you must continue to move forward and not look back, and discover that you can do even more as part of your destiny.

To keep up the momentum, recognize that the journey is never over. Keep up the newfound momentum gained from setting and achieving Destiny Goals and do your best to keep it up!

Once we reach our goals we can be tempted to shift back into an old way of thinking, but this is the critical juncture that will define the rest of your progress towards a bigger future. Celebrate the big win and then either expand your Destiny Goal or create a brand new one.

Lasting success is not found in the completion of a goal; success is found by the change we make within during the journey. By working towards a goal we change for the better, as goals require us to learn skills along the way.

Nourish your newfound skills by keeping up the momentum. Relish the win and be proud of your victory. But don't become complacent and let your skills die off. Keep putting your nose to the grindstone and keep working at this thing we call life.

Continue to work on your goals, skills, and aim to seek deeper meaning in life. After laying a firm foundation, and learning how to keep up the pace with momentum strategies, it's time now to delve into the *why*.

Your personal "why" will keep you going well beyond any other initiative.

It's a goal of mine to inspire you to dig deep into the subject of this last section in order to find your ultimate purpose. I want you to be a person that will never lose steam and will know how to keep rolling along.

Let's dive into the why to make sure we never again lose momentum.

UNLEASH YOUR UNBOUNDED POTENTIAL

I am a firm believer in people. I believe that each person has unique gifts that, if used the right way, can change the world. I firmly believe in you.

No matter what your current circumstances, you have the capacity to make a difference. It doesn't matter your age, your skills, or how many kids you have.

Reject the belief that you can only do so much. Believe in yourself, and don't be limited by a nagging doubt that you aren't good enough.

A fully-grown male elephant can be prevented from wandering with the use of a simple rope. When younger, these elephants are restricted with a chain they cannot break. This limiting belief then extends to their older years when owners are able to restrict movement with a small piece of twine. The elephant does not believe it can escape, so it doesn't bother to try. A six-ton beast is held in place by a tiny piece of rope solely because it *believes* it can't escape. How amazing, but also how sad!

This is the power of limiting beliefs. And unfortunately this story rings true for us too. It shows us how the limitations we envision can prevent us from doing anything epic with our lives. We become our own self-fulfilling prophecy by believing we live in the unbreakable box of poverty, physical limitations, or societal pressures.

To say goodbye to those limiting beliefs and springboard into life change, I recommend the following three practical baby steps:

1) Ask yourself: What's the number-one roadblock I am facing today? Write down your answer in your journal and ponder why you think it's stopping you. Whether it's finances, lack of education or experience, or you don't think you have what it takes, identification is the first step.

2) Change your language from "I can't get past this" to "I'll schedule time this week to take the first step towards overcoming this obstacle." Tell yourself that you will indeed move beyond seemingly insurmountable obstacles as long as you take the right steps.

3) Brainstorm a list of further action steps to continue to move you beyond the roadblock. I mentioned brainstorming earlier in this book, but I consistently find that it's the best way to create a deluge of actionable ideas that fit your lifestyle, goals, and circumstances.

Once you decide you are valuable and make a plan of action to conquer your limiting beliefs, you will discover your very own Volcanic Momentum.

Refer back to the list above when you need to, and before long you will become an expert at getting things done.

I've seen too many people wonder at what could be without ever finding out. If you feel stuck, the most likely decision that you need to make is to jump in and try something new. It's OKAY and inevitable that you will fail. Remember, failure is one of the keys to momentum!

Is staying in the same place, doing the same things, feeling the same old way really what you want? No, what we want is to get past what always stops us and get those goals.

Consider people like Cornel Hrisca-Munn. He was born with no forearms and a deformed leg. He was left in an institution unwanted, rejected, and with little chance at survival. He was then shown kindness and survived. At age six, Cornel rode his tricycle four miles around Gheluvelt Park in Worcester, raising 8,500 pounds for a young Romanian boy with leukemia. Now he is a famous YouTube star for his drumming abilities of all things. I hear you say "What!? Seriously!?" But it's true.

And did you know that at the age of fifteen Charlize Theron witnessed her mother kill her abusive father in self-defense? She didn't let this horrible event stymie her from going on to become the first South African actress to win an Academy Award (and she was great in *The Italian Job!*). She was able to move past tragedy and find major success by not letting a life event form her destiny and instead choosing to reach a big goal. She now runs a charity called the *Charlize Theron Africa Outreach Project (CTAOP)*[16] which invests in African youth to keep themselves safe from HIV/AIDS.

I share these incredible stories to prove that every individual has limitless potential. If you face adversity, that potential is not diminished, it's brightened! Sometimes the most powerful words come from those that have passed through the darkness themselves.

The pastor of my church is very open about his not-so-bright past. He struggled with drinking, promiscuity, and drugs while growing up. In his vulnerability he invites people of all walks of life to be welcomed into the church and to not feel judged for where they have been.

---

16   Charlize Theron Africa Outreach Project, charlizeafricaoutreach.org.

My respect and admiration for him is never higher than when he is vulnerable. He desires for people to tap into their potential no matter what they have done, because he knows the power and impact of those that have lived with mistakes.

I've never been a heavy drinker, or a drug user. Heck, I've never even smoked a cigarette (and I just used the word "heck"). But I've done other things I am not so proud of, as have we all. But no matter what we have done, no matter our circumstances, no matter how much baggage we have now, we can shrug it off and start again.

Nelson Mandela says this:

"There is no passion to be found in playing small—In settling for a life that is less than the one you are capable of living."

Throughout this book I shared ways that you can increase your personal growth momentum, but none of it will work if you don't truly believe in yourself. Now is your chance to take action on the list above and ensure that you never lose steam.

You don't need to be an expert to start doing something. Everyone starts somewhere, but the key is to start and then build momentum over time.

You don't need to be the best, but you do need to be *you* and give enough of a damn to make a difference. (He went from "heck" all the way to "damn," he must really be serious. Darn tootin' I am!)

Are You Willing to Bet on You?

We are so willing to bet on those we love and support them with undying loyalty. When was the last time you were willing to bet on yourself?

Believe in yourself and what you can accomplish and win big for not only you, but for those around you as well.

Believe that you can accomplish those big Destiny Goals (because you can) and give yourself the credit you deserve (because you do). There are enough naysayers and negative people out there that will get you down if you let them. Don't even give them the chance. If you want to learn a new language, travel to a new place, or take up kickboxing, do it!

It may not work out, but the more you can put yourself in situations in which you aren't 100% comfortable, the more you will grow.

As a 100% Myers-Briggs rated introvert, I know that every time I go out to hang with friends I am growing. Every awkward situation grows my ability to detect and avoid future awkward situations.

I don't let this life roadblock stop me; instead I embrace it for what it is and do my best to get past it.

Stand up, release your potential, and play big today by:

- Saying yes to a new challenge. Put yourself out there. Grow into your destiny.

- Making a small positive change in your lifestyle today.

- Calling your mother or grandmother. This one is always good for positive vibes and good graces, and to be encouraged to keep up your good work.

- Dreaming big with a loved one. Brainstorm the myriad ways you can change the world, and then get to it!

- Learning to risk big, lose well, and smile through it all.

Believe in yourself and the world will change before your eyes.

LEAVING NORMAL BEHIND

The other day I pulled into a parking lot and noticed something odd. Every car was parked in the same direction! How cool, right? Except I ruined it. I parked in the opposite direction.

And I was so freakin' happy about it.

As I deliberately parked facing the opposite direction, Miranda sighed and gave a slight chuckle at my actions. I proclaimed myself the king of non-conformity as she just got out of the car and grabbed her weights and proceeded to boot camp. I wore a huge goofy grin as I grabbed my own dumbbells and walked to our workout.

Actions like these make me feel great about the world and my place in it. I love those little moments that break up what can be a monotonous life at times.

From sharing one car with my wife, to working as a freelance writer, to littering the walls of our apartment with whiteboards, we are leaving normal behind and we love it.

Why Leave Normal Behind?

Mark Batterson (A well-known Christian author, and my personal favorite writer) says:

"We must stop living as if the purpose of life is to arrive safely at death."

I get pumped up every time I think about the above quote, so much so that it's become my life mantra of sorts.

We are not meant to all wear the same shoes, park the same way, or do the same things with our lives.

We are meant for much, much more.

If we dream big, take huge risks, and take monumental action, the world could and would be a better place. As I shared in the last chapter, each of us has within us ridiculous potential.

Normal means:

- Not setting goals (less than 3% of Americans write down their goals).
- Never having enough energy for the important moments in life.
- Not looking for deeper meaning…

By reading this book, you have set yourself up for success by the mere fact that you're considering what your life goals should be! And by adding Destiny Goals to your life!? You just left normal in the dust. Congratulations.

But it doesn't stop there. You need to know that doing things outside the norm comes with consequences to consider other than potential parking violations.

I read a blog article once about social media woes when it comes to sharing about entrepreneurship and owning a business.

The author shared that when we post a status like "I got a job!' we could get a hundred likes, and if we post a status that says, "I am starting my own business!" We get relative crickets.

People want to conform. We ultimately want to be liked and accepted, and we want others to feel the way we do. We want to be comfortable and feel included. The problem with our proclivity to conform is that we pull others down with us if we are feeling low.

We Need to Challenge This Line of Thinking

Don't pull others down with you. Build them up.

Next time something great happens to a friend, consider:

- Being truly happy for a blogging buddy that suddenly gets a mass amount of traffic, instead of silently wishing that the traffic had come to you instead.
- When a good friend loses fifty pounds, meaningfully congratulate them instead of focusing on the ten you have to lose to get beach ready.
- If a friend gets their dream job (that also happens to be *your* dream job), meditate on good thoughts for them, instead of immediately planning their demise.

We have all at one time or another secretly wished for failure for someone else because in some sick way it would make us feel better about ourselves and our own plight.

I know that I have done this, even if I am not proud to admit it.

This is the true danger of conformity and where it gets extremely tricky to live outside the box.

Non-conformity means being willing to do things others are not. It means not caring what the majority think if you know in your heart that it's right or good. It's about not caving in to peer pressure.

This includes being there for other people and lifting them up. It means providing people with a helping hand when they need it, even if we think it will end up bringing us down.

To me, the simple act of parking differently than all other cars around me served as a reminder of this thought process. It's good and right to think differently than others, not because we want to be rebellious, but because we strive for growth and change. I realize it literally means nothing to park the other way, but it means much in remembering to think for yourself.

We need to remember that just because others are doing it doesn't mean it's right.

We need to challenge the thought process behind every decision we make and be sure that *we are making it*, not a heavily influenced voice in the back of our heads.

The "groupthink" mentality is truly dangerous, and it can lead us to make some really bad decisions, like going to college when you have no idea what your major is going to be (*raises hand).

Think critically of your own beliefs and be aware of the effect that others' opinions have on you. Accept good advice and well-meaning feedback from others, but always run it through your personal filter first.

Trust your instincts first before giving into societal pressures. Cultivate a growing desire to break free from the norm and you will find contentment waiting for you.

To quote from the movie *Dead Poets Society:*

"Boys, you must strive to find your own voice. Because the longer you wait

to begin, the less likely you are to find it at all. Thoreau said, "Most men lead lives of quiet desperation." Don't be resigned to that. Break out!"

Moving Forward

To leave normal behind, I recommend the following three action steps:

1) Think and act like a nonconformist by doing things differently than others. Wake up a little earlier, write a little bit more, park the wrong way, go on a forty-day fast, or quit watching TV. Get to know yourself better and discover just how much more you can push yourself to the limit.

2) Find your passion and pursue it with all of your heart. Be willing to sacrifice and say goodbye to hobbies, objects, and even relationships if necessary. We only have one life so we might as well live it to the fullest. Don't get stuck feeling stuck.

3) Listen to the podcast I co-host with my wife Miranda, *Leaving Normal Behind*. We talk all things nonconformity and getting more out of life. It is our heart to help people get just a little bit more out of life. And oh yeah, we are goofy because life is fun.

Good luck as you move forward in your journey to non-conformity. You will find that the more you do that is outside the norm, the more you will learn about yourself and the world around you.

O CAPTAIN! MY CAPTAIN!

*"I went to the woods because I wished to live deliberately,
to front only the essential facts of life, and see if I could not
learn what it had to teach, and not, when I came to die,
discover that I had not lived."*

—Henry David Thoreau

I still get chills every time I watch *Dead Poets Society*.

In arguably the most climactic moment in cinematic history, Todd Anderson stands upon his desk and proclaims "O Captain! My Captain!" to his teacher, John Keating. As the music rises and tension builds to this one moment, I am enraptured by Todd's choice to break free from his fear of breaking rules and declare his reverence and thanks to his mentor.

Other boys, under a similar struggle of right and wrong, are bolstered by Todd's courage and choose to stand as well. As Mr. Keating stands there and accepts the acknowledgements, his love and admiration for his students is felt more than heard as he utters a soft "Thank you, boys."

This one epic moment of non-conformity and doing the right thing in the face of adversity has defined my life since the first time I watched the movie.

I believe we are all called at times to shout "O Captain! My Captain!"

from the hilltops, but also to whisper it during the quiet struggles of everyday life.

Life is hard, sometimes unbearably so, and serving a higher purpose gets me through. What is your higher purpose in life? Who or what is your Captain?

After reading the book *Cosmos* by Carl Sagan I was blown away by his vast depth of scientific knowledge. The book was an incredible look at the vastness of time and space. We are infinitesimal specks and only a mere blip on the radar of time. Yet with all of his genius and understanding of the cosmos, Carl missed an important point.

Genius and progress means nothing if not born of a greater purpose beyond mere scientific advancement. Science is an amazing tool that we can use for the betterment of our lives, but it fails to give our lives deeper meaning.

Knowing my higher purpose and my Destiny Goals has defined my life in powerful and meaningful ways. Without this truth, life seems to be meaningless. Without a higher power and greater purpose to guide my steps and direct my path, what's the point? I don't want to set and reach goals for my happiness alone.

Your perspective might be different and that's okay. I have not shared your experiences, your joys, or your pain. We all are in different places and on different life paths. Some people have it really easy, and others have a rough go.

I do, however, encourage you to question. That's it. That's all I ask and suggest. Question what you believe. Questioning is one of the most powerful tools to learning and growth, and if you can master it, you will soar.

I hate a sales pitch or being convinced of anything and I know most people feel the same so I won't try to sell you here. We don't truly believe something unless WE choose it ourselves.

It's my goal to urge you to question everything and think outside of the box. If it leads you away from my own conclusions, then maybe I need to continue to question things as well. There is so much we don't know!

If this book encourages you and instilled in you a desire to ask big questions of your life, then I declare it a success, whether or not you agree with me.

It's through questioning our purpose, goals, and direction that we grow. It's through contemplation that we find true and lasting momentum. Without stopping to think and wonder, we will never get anywhere.

Our spiritual viewpoints are often the most difficult to question or even talk about, especially in today's culture. Since it's my mission to reduce passivity and lead people to action, I pose these questions here.

If you can question your spiritual beliefs and seek additional answers on this topic, you can go forth and grow in other areas as well.

Starting with the most important question (your purpose) gives you the ability to grow and expand in other ways.

All I ask is that you question. Read books on science, religion, and other worldviews. Don't relegate yourself to the cop-out of believing we can't know and then never questioning the idea.

If we don't seek the truth, it might never come to us. Seek out the truth and challenge yourself to know more.

For me, I know what my higher purpose is. I encourage you to seek out yours and to question what purpose your life is fulfilling beyond you.

Question and Seek Above All.

The content within this book will be 100% more applicable if you can position yourself to question these things:

- Question your motives and goals
- Question your past choices
- Question your beliefs and commitments
- Question your desires, wants, and needs
- Question your priorities

Position yourself with an attitude of questioning and a willingness to make a change. I'm not one to say that something will definitely work for you over another, but the only way you'll know for sure is if you try new things.

Don't believe for a second that you are stuck. Break free by asking questions and seeking answers.

Explosive growth and positive change come with growing pains and major struggles. They go together like spaghetti and meatballs. Know that the pain is worth it in the end.

Think about your own beliefs and seek answers about your beliefs as you build momentum toward your destiny. Life will open before you in ways you would have never expected.

Sustaining Volcanic Momentum: Deep Thinking Questions As You Finish this Book:

- What do you believe in?

- What is most important to you?

- How does your everyday life reflect the answers to the last two questions?

Conclusion:
TAKE ACTION NOW

"If you want to walk on water, you've got to get out of the boat"
—John Ortberg[17]

Reading this book means nothing if you don't take action. I'm obsessed with action, and for good reason. Without action nothing will change in this world.

I love reading and I think that books are the number-one way we can find personal growth. That being said, if you finish this book (or any book for that matter) and don't apply at least one of the learned principles to your life, what was the point of reading?

Inaction and passivity are what's slowly killing us and preventing us from fulfilling our destiny. We must learn how to put passivity behind us and take determined action.

To that end, I'd like to share **17 takeaways** from this book that will inspire you to take action in order to grow. This is only a small snippet of the topics covered, but if you get stuck, start with something in this list. Choose one of these to apply right away:

---

17   *If You Want to Walk on Water, You've Got to Get Out of the Boat A Six Session Journey on Learning to Trust God.* Zondervan, 2014.

1) Lay a firm foundation for the future. Build a solid base of varied goals and then build the motivation necessary to complete them.

2) Set up tracking for your goals so you know where you've been, where you are, and what you want to accomplish in the future.

3) Give yourself a quick win to gain that first little chug of momentum. The train won't start rolling along unless it can get a little send off. Set yourself up for success by taking a positive baby step.

4) Don't take yourself too seriously. Laugh at yourself often and put yourself in uncomfortable situations so you can grow. This involves trying new things and not being afraid to be embarrassed. Life is better when we can find the humor in the egg on our faces.

5) Don't beat yourself up or be too hard on yourself. Don't get upset with what you've done up to this point in your life. You can always start fresh. The best part about life is that it's never too late to set and crush Destiny Goals.

6) Move forward. Remember that you are never neutral. You are either moving backwards away from a goal or towards completion.

7) Ask a ton of questions. Ask yourself questions. Ask others questions about yourself and about them. Question everything in order to truly grow.

8) Adopt a long-term mindset of energy conservation. Know that your big Destiny Goals will NOT be completed overnight. Have patience, young padawan. Your dreams will come true, in time.

9) Fail often and fail hard. Failure is the number-one way to grow quickly. Learn from your mistakes and grow.

10) Reject passivity and don't waste the precious and finite resource of time. Always be taking action steps towards your goals in order to see them through to completion.

11) Master your priorities in order to find time for the things that you really want to do and for the people that you really want to grow with. Create margin in your life so you can breathe and find room to grow.

12) Build a community around you to help propel you skywards, reaching heights you wouldn't believe possible.

13) Do things for others. Get in the habit of reaching out and you will be blessed beyond measure. Learn to set aside yourself and instead spend time doing for others, praying for others, and thinking about others.

14) Read more. Read to succeed.

15) Admit that you are probably not living out your maximum potential right now. Commit to working on your personal growth and do the best that you can with every day that you have.

16) Find your purpose by living out your *why*. Figure out what it is you're living for by asking life's tough questions, of yourselves and others. If you don't know exactly what you are supposed to do, get busy doing *something* in the meantime. Most of us don't know exactly what we're called to do. That's okay; still work towards a direction while you patiently wait for it to be revealed.

17) Take action on what you learn. Don't even think about closing this book without taking an action step towards a better future. Don't go to bed tonight without moving the needle forward one inch.

I will leave you with one final quote from *Dead Poets Society:*

"We don't read and write poetry because it's cute. We read and write poetry because we are members of the human race. And the human race is filled with passion. And medicine, law, business, engineering, these are noble pursuits and necessary to sustain life. But poetry, beauty, romance, love, these are what we stay alive for. To quote from Whitman, "O me! O life!... of the questions of these recurring; of the endless trains of the faithless... of cities filled with the foolish; what good amid these, O me, O life?" Answer: That you are here—that life exists, and identity; that the powerful play goes on and you may contribute a verse. That the powerful play *goes on* and you may contribute a verse. What will your verse be?"

—John Keating

Did you just get goosebumps? Good, I know I do every single time I read or hear that quote.

Oh what a powerful verse you can be. Take action today and change the world, friend!

A QUICK FAVOR?

Before you go, can I ask you for a quick favor? Would you please review this book?

Reviews are very important for authors, and your honest feedback can help others find me. Do me a solid and leave a review today on Amazon by following this link:

www.JMRing.com/review-volcanic-momentum

Thank you for reading, and thank you so much for being a part of this adventure.

—Jordan

ABOUT THE AUTHOR

Jordan Ring might seem like an intergalactic task-ninja, but he's an authorpreneur at heart. As good as he is with words, his primary goal is to help you live a life of less talk and more action. When he isn't busy writing, blogging, or podcasting, Jordan is also the book-marketing and launch guru for clients over at his second home, Archangel Ink. And that's not all: He's also a freelance copywriter, writing coach, consultant—and anything else he can do to keep the lights on and coffee comin'.

His hobbies include playing on Trello boards, watching Marvel movies, drinking iced coffee, and hanging out with his amazing wife, Miranda. Together, they run a podcast called *Freedom-Cast: Leaving Normal Behind.* You can see what all he's up to on his site at www.JMRing.com.